mini **FOR ORGANS, PIANOS & ELECTRONIC KEYBOARDS** E-Z PLAY TODAY

8

Over the Rainbow

G

ISBN 978-1-4950-7725-8

HAL•LEONARD®

7777 W. Bluemound Rd. P.O. Box 13819 Milwaukee, WI 53213

E-Z Play® Today Music Notation © 1975 by HAL LEONARD LLC
E-Z PLAY and EASY ELECTRONIC KEYBOARD MUSIC are registered trademarks of HAL LEONARD LLC.

Visit Hal Leonard Online at
www.halleonard.com

At Last

Registration 3
Rhythm: Ballad or Swing

Lyric by Mack Gordon
Music by Harry Warren

At
last _____ my love has come a-
last _____ the skies a-bove are

long, _____ my lone-ly days are o - ver _____
blue, _____ my heart was wrapped in clo - ver _____

_____ and life is like a song. _____ At
_____ the night I looked at

you.   I found a dream that I can

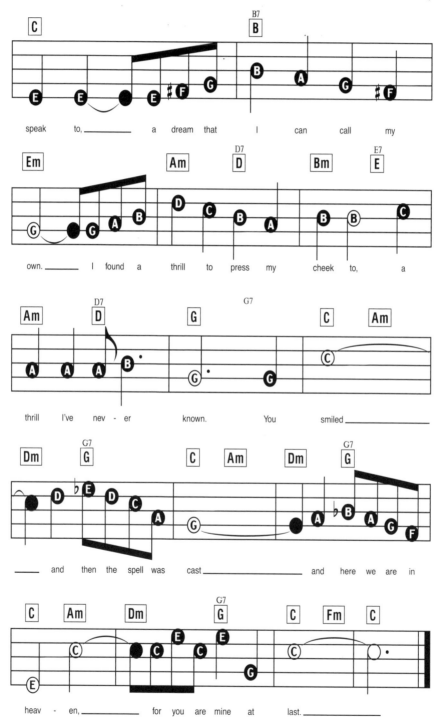

Cute

Registration 7
Rhythm: Swing or Fox Trot

Music by Neal Hefti
Words by Stanley Styne

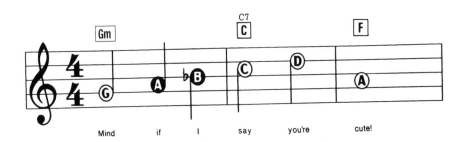

Mind   if   I   say   you're   cute!

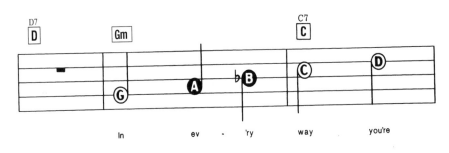

In   ev - 'ry   way   you're

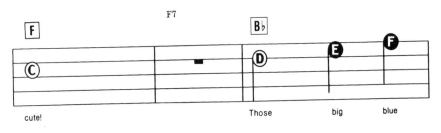

cute!   Those   big   blue

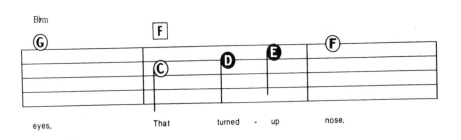

eyes,   That   turned - up   nose,

7

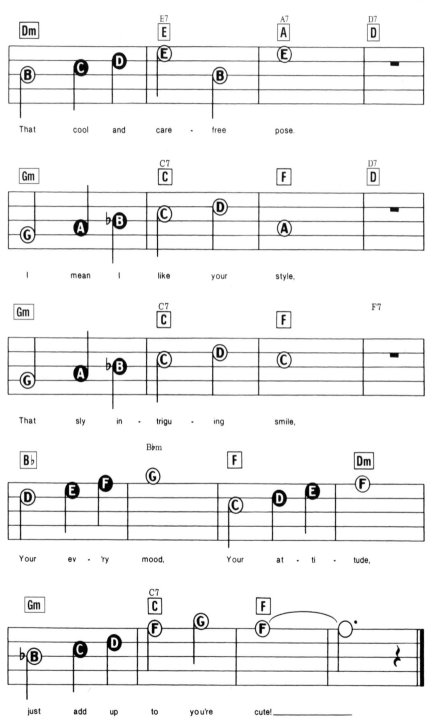

Feeling Good

from THE ROAR OF THE GREASEPAINT – THE SMELL OF THE CROWD

Registration 8
Rhythm: 4/4 Ballad or Rock

Words and Music by Leslie Bricusse
and Anthony Newley

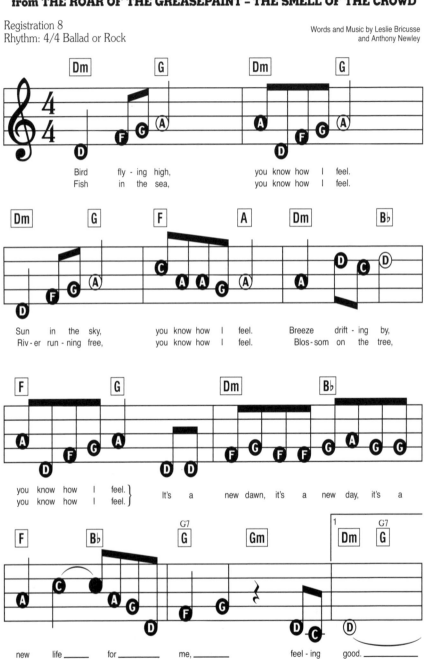

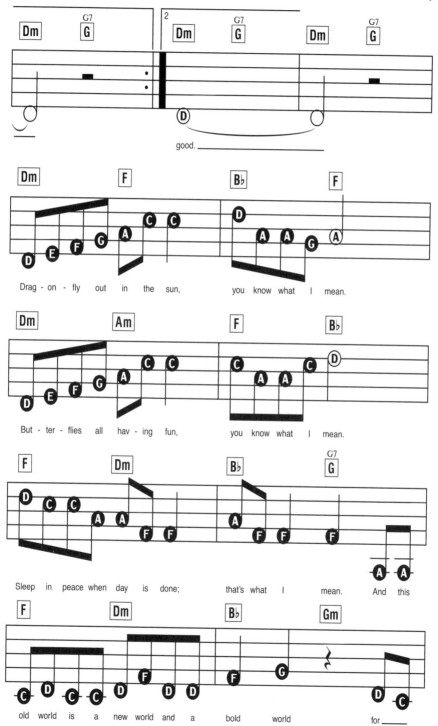

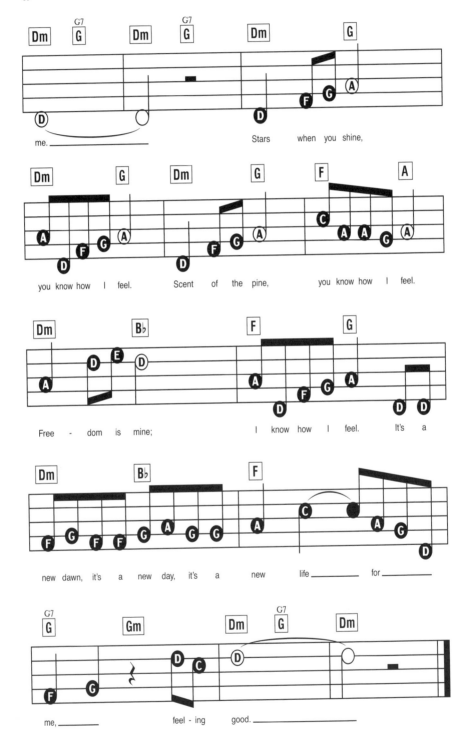

Good Morning Starshine

from the Broadway Musical Production HAIR

Registration 4
Rhythm: Rock

Words by James Rado
and Gerome Ragni
Music by Galt MacDermot

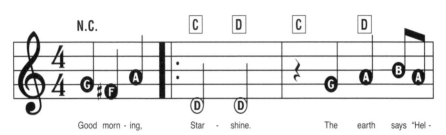

Good morn - ing, Star - shine. The earth says "Hel -

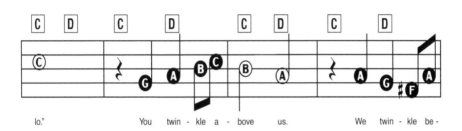

lo." You twin - kle a - bove us. We twin - kle be -

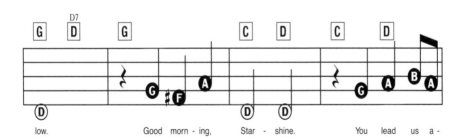

low. Good morn - ing, Star - shine. You lead us a -

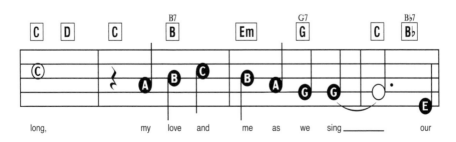

long, my love and me as we sing_____ our

12

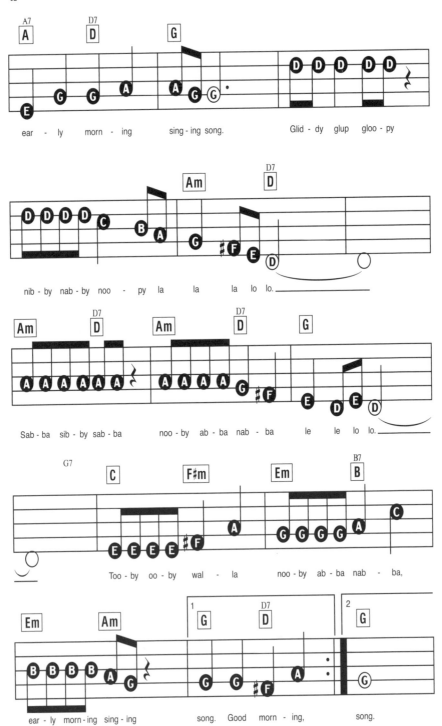

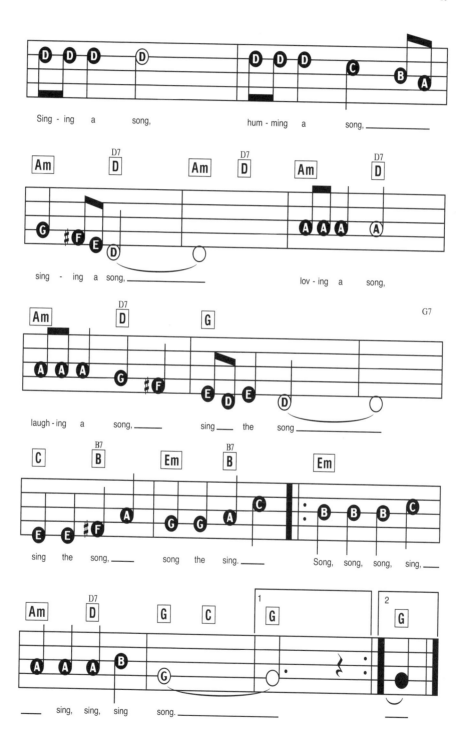

Gentle Rain

Registration 4
Rhythm: Bossa Nova or Latin

Music by Luiz Bonfa
Words by Matt Dubey

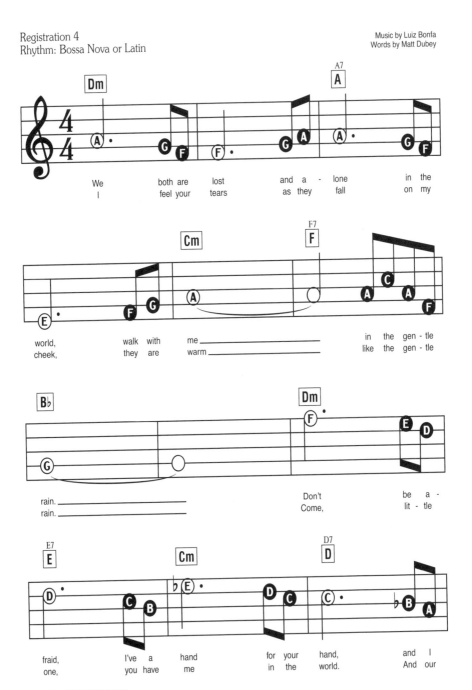

We / I
both are / feel your
lost / tears
and a - lone / as they
fall
in the / on my

world, / cheek,
walk with / they are
me / warm
in the gen - tle / like the gen - tle

rain. / rain.
Don't / Come,
be a - / lit - tle

fraid, / one,
I've a / you have
hand / me
for your / in the
hand, / world.
and I / And our

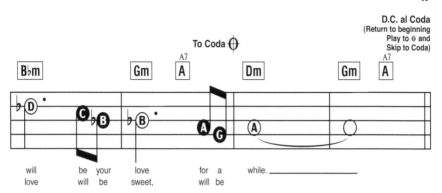

To Coda

D.C. al Coda
(Return to beginning
Play to ⊕ and
Skip to Coda)

will / love   be / will   your / be   love / sweet,   for / will   a / be   while.

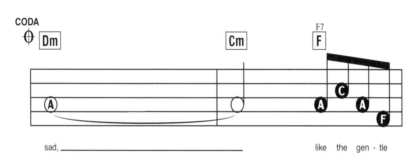

CODA

sad,   like the gen - tle

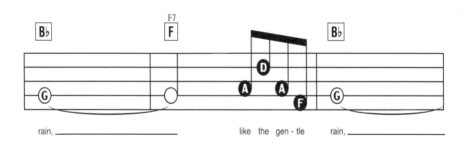

rain,   like the gen - tle   rain,

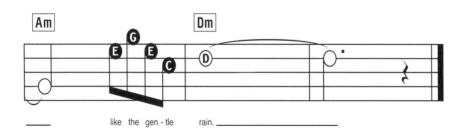

like the gen - tle   rain.

Hello, Dolly!
from HELLO, DOLLY!

Registration 5
Rhythm: Swing

Music and Lyric by
Jerry Herman

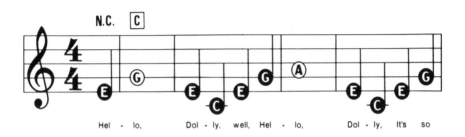

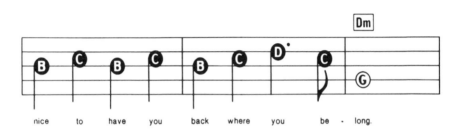

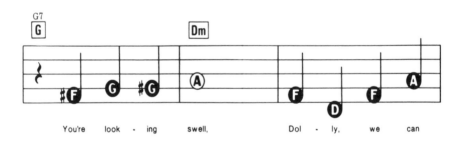

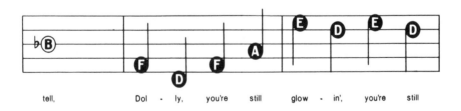

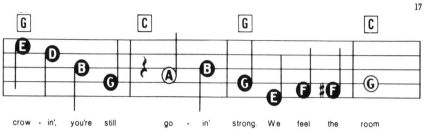

crow - in', you're still go - in' strong. We feel the room

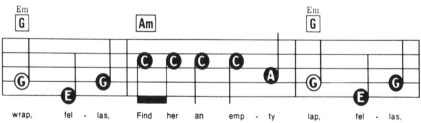

sway - in', for the band's play - in' one of your old fa - v'rite

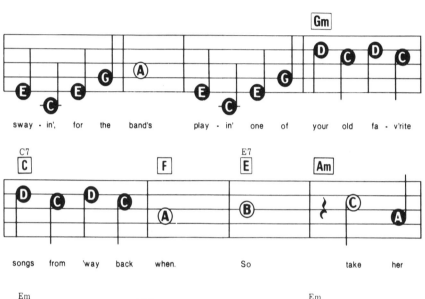

songs from 'way back when. So take her

wrap, fel - las, Find her an emp - ty lap, fel - las,

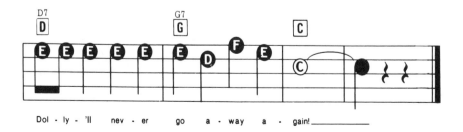

Dol - ly - 'll nev - er go a - way a - gain!_____

Hey, Look Me Over
from WILDCAT

Registration 7
Rhythm: 6/8 March

Music by Cy Coleman
Lyrics by Carolyn Leigh

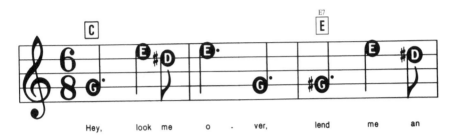

Hey, look me o - ver, lend me an

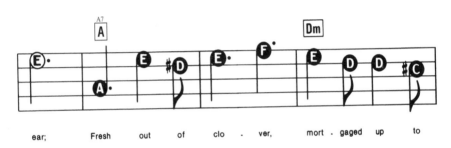

ear; Fresh out of clo - ver, mort - gaged up to

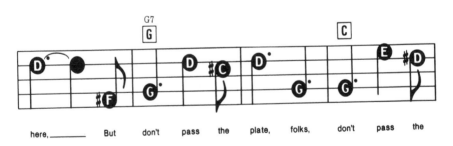

here,_____ But don't pass the plate, folks, don't pass the

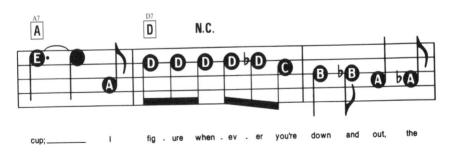

cup;_____ I fig - ure when - ev - er you're down and out, the

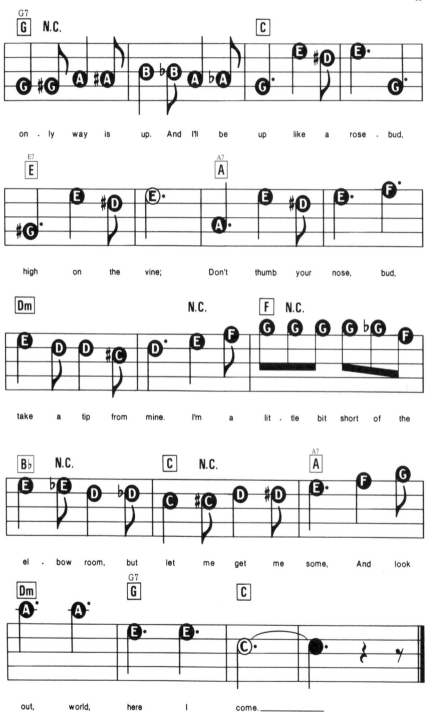

on - ly   way   is   up.   And   I'll   be   up   like   a   rose - bud,

high   on   the   vine;   Don't   thumb   your   nose,   bud,

take   a   tip   from   mine.   I'm   a   lit - tle   bit   short   of   the

el - bow   room,   but   let   me   get   me   some,   And   look

out,   world,   here   I   come.____

I Put a Spell on You

Registration 4
Rhythm: 6/8 Waltz

Words and Music by
Jay Hawkins

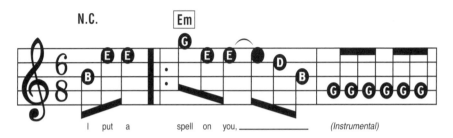

I put a   spell on you, _____   (Instrumental)

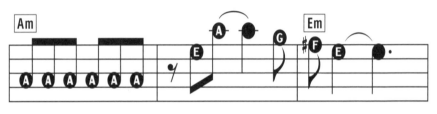

be - cause ____ you're   mine. _____

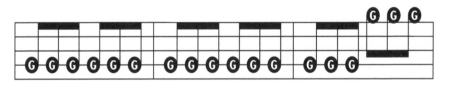

(Instrumental)   You bet - ter

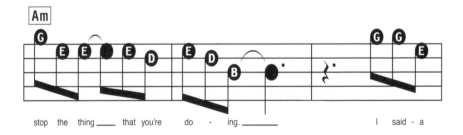

stop   the   thing ____ that you're   do - ing. _____   I   said - a

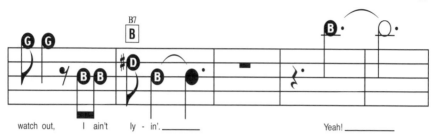

watch out, I ain't ly - in'._____ Yeah!_____

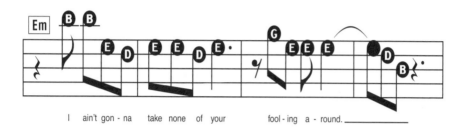

I ain't gon - na take none of your fool - ing a - round._____

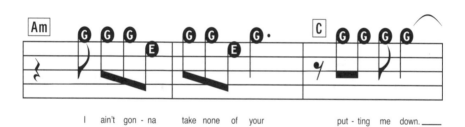

I ain't gon - na take none of your put - ting me down.____

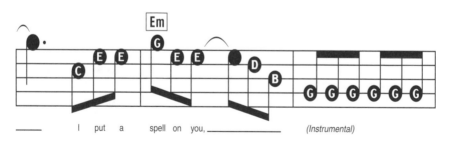

_____ I put a spell on you,_____ (Instrumental)

be - cause____ you're mine. ____ Whoa whoa,

22

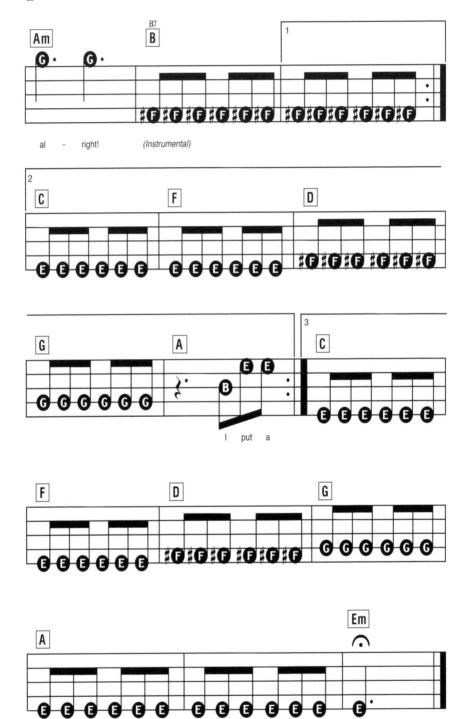

Minnie the Moocher

Registration 2
Rhythm: Fox Trot or Swing

Words and Music by Cab Calloway
and Irving Mills

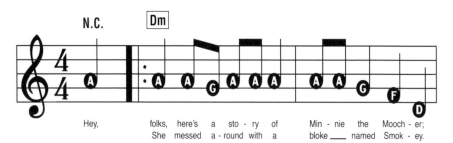

Hey,   folks, here's a sto - ry of   Min - nie the Mooch - er;
She messed a - round with a   bloke ___ named Smok - ey.

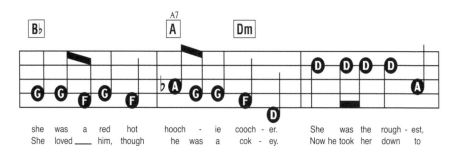

she was a red hot hooch - ie cooch - er.   She was the rough - est,
She loved ___ him, though he was a cok - ey.   Now he took her down to

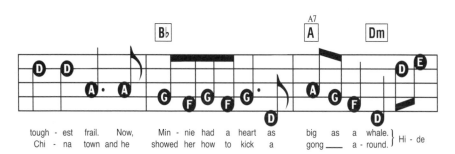

tough - est frail. Now,   Min - nie had a heart as   big as a whale. } Hi - de
Chi - na town and he   showed her how to kick a   gong ___ a - round. } Hi - de

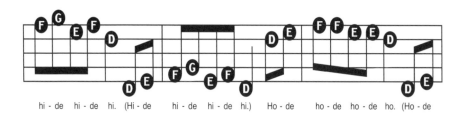

hi - de   hi - de hi.   (Hi - de   hi - de   hi - de hi.)   Ho - de   ho - de ho - de ho.   (Ho - de

24

ho - de   ho - de   ho.)   He - de   he - de   he - de   he - de   he. (He - de   he - de   he - de   he - de   he.)   Hi - de

A   Dm   A   Dm

hi - de   hi - de   hi.   (Hi - de   hi - de   hi - de   hi.)

Bb7   A7   1   Bb7   A7   2   Bb7   A7
Bb   A   Dm   Bb   A   Bb   A

(Instrumental)

Now

Dm   Bb

she had   a   dream   a - bout   a   king   from   Swe - den.   He   gave   her   things   that

A7
A   Dm

she ___ was   need - in'.   Now he   built   her   a   home   of   gold   and   steel   and   a

Rhythm: Double-Time (♩=♩)

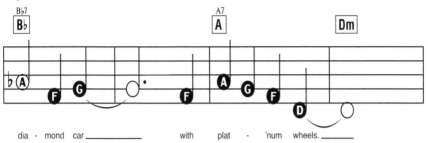

dia - mond car_____ with plat - 'num wheels._____

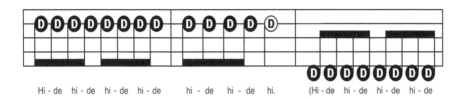

Hi - de hi - de hi - de hi - de   hi - de hi - de hi.   (Hi - de hi - de hi - de hi - de

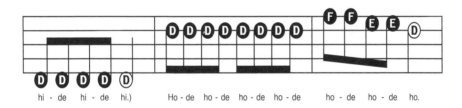

hi - de hi - de hi.)   Ho - de ho - de ho - de ho - de   ho - de ho - de ho.

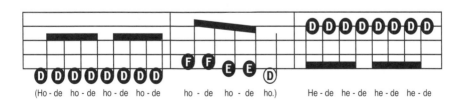

(Ho - de ho - de ho - de ho - de   ho - de ho - de ho.)   He - de he - de he - de he - de

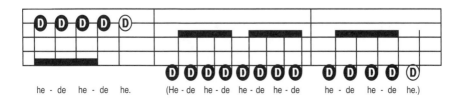

he - de he - de he.   (He - de he - de he - de he - de   he - de he - de he.)

26

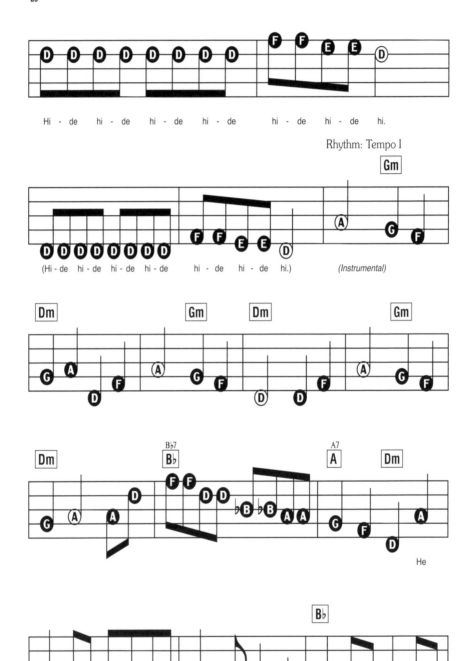

Hi - de hi - de hi - de hi - de hi - de hi - de hi.

Rhythm: Tempo I

(Hi - de hi - de hi - de hi - de hi - de hi - de hi.) *(Instrumental)*

He

gave her his town - house and his rac - ing hors - es. Each meal she ate was a

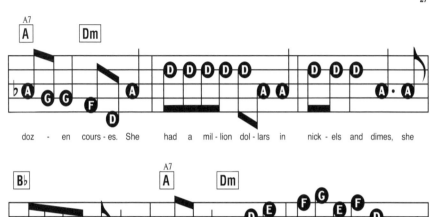

doz - en cours - es. She had a mil - lion dol - lars in nick - els and dimes, she

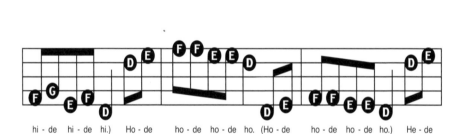

sat a - round and count - ed one mil - lion times. Hi - de hi - de hi - de hi. (Hi - de

hi - de hi - de hi.) Ho - de ho - de ho - de ho. (Ho - de ho - de ho - de ho.) He - de

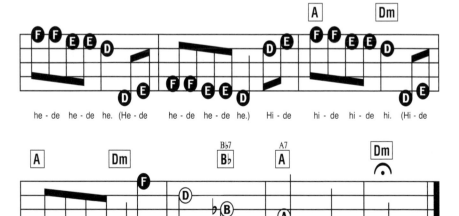

he - de he - de he. (He - de he - de he - de he.) Hi - de hi - de hi - de hi. (Hi - de

hi - de hi - de hi.) Poor Min, poor Min, poor Min.

I Shall Be Released

Registration 4
Rhythm: Country Rock or 8-Beat

Words and Music by
Bob Dylan

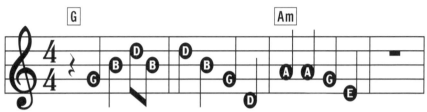

1. They say ev - 'ry man must need pro - tec - tion, _____
2., 3. *(See additional lyrics)*

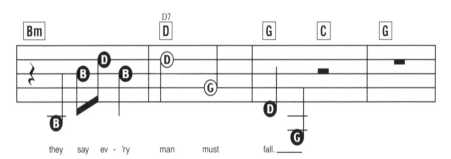

they say ev - 'ry man must fall. _____

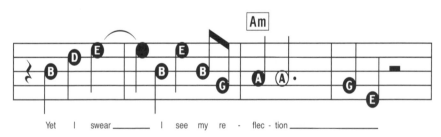

Yet I swear _____ I see my re - flec - tion _____

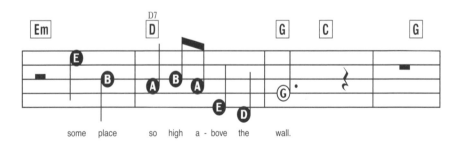

some place so high a - bove the wall.

Chorus

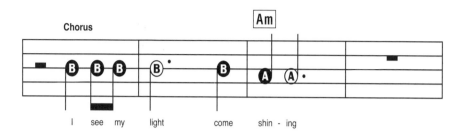

I see my light come shin - ing

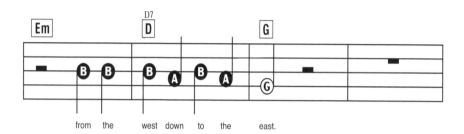

from the west down to the east.

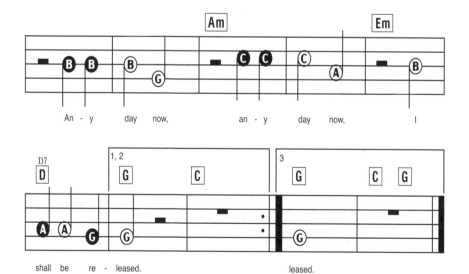

An - y day now, an - y day now, I

shall be re - leased. leased.

Additional Lyrics

2. Down here next to me in this lonely crowd
Is a man who swears he's not to blame.
All day long I hear him cry so loud,
Calling out that he's been framed.
Chorus

3. They say ev'rything can be replaced,
Yet ev'ry distance is not near.
So I remember ev'ry face
Of ev'ry man who put me here.
Chorus

I Wanna Be Around

Registration 4
Rhythm: Swing or Jazz

Words by Johnny Mercer
Music by Sadie Vimmerstedt

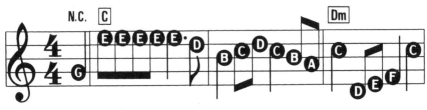

I wan-na be a-round to pick up the piec-es, when some-bod-y breaks your

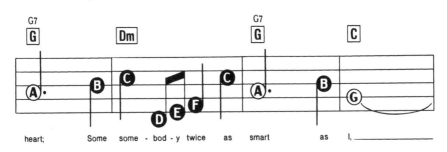

heart; Some some-bod-y twice as smart as I,

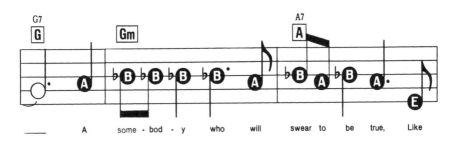

A some-bod-y who will swear to be true, Like

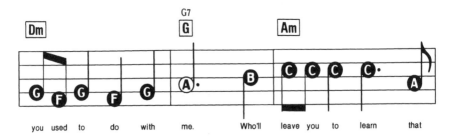

you used to do with me. Who'll leave you to learn that

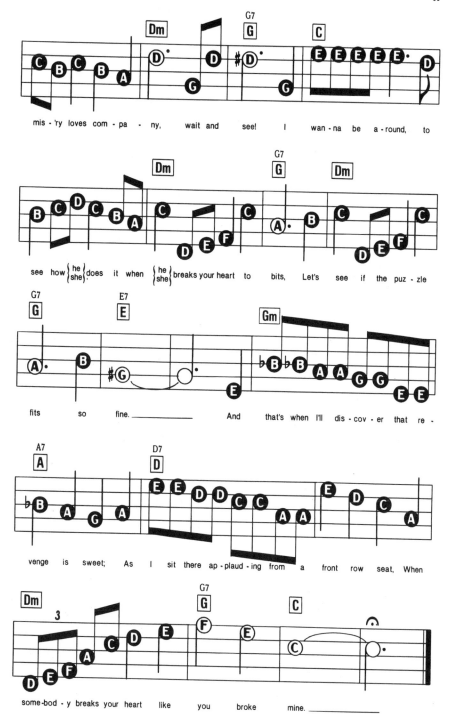

I'd Like to Teach the World to Sing

Registration 4
Rhythm: Rock

Words and Music by Bill Backer,
Roquel Davis, Roger Cook
and Roger Greenaway

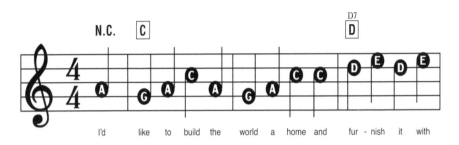

I'd like to build the world a home and fur - nish it with

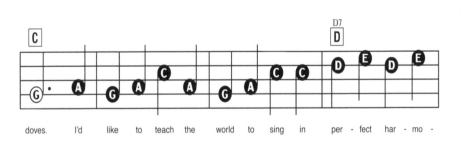

love, grow ap - ple trees and hon - ey bees and snow - white tur - tle -

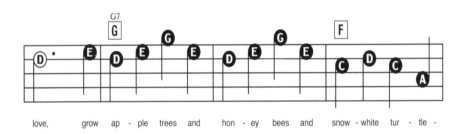

doves. I'd like to teach the world to sing in per - fect har - mo -

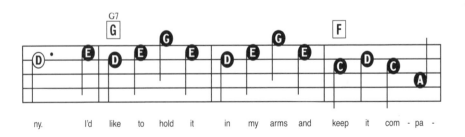

ny. I'd like to hold it in my arms and keep it com - pa -

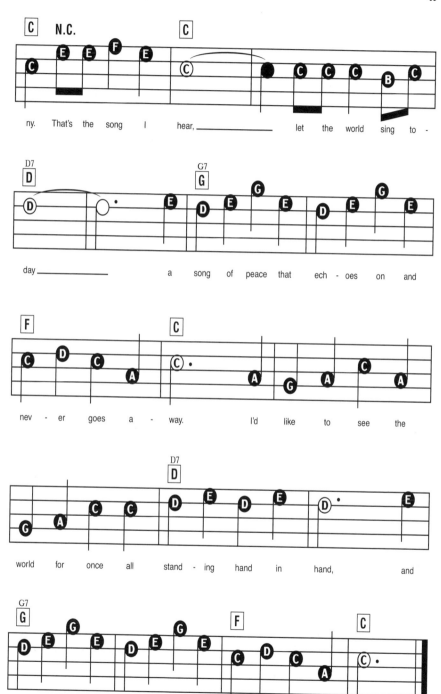

I've Got a Gal in Kalamazoo

Registration 2
Rhythm: Swing or Jazz

Words by Mack Gordon
Music by Harry Warren

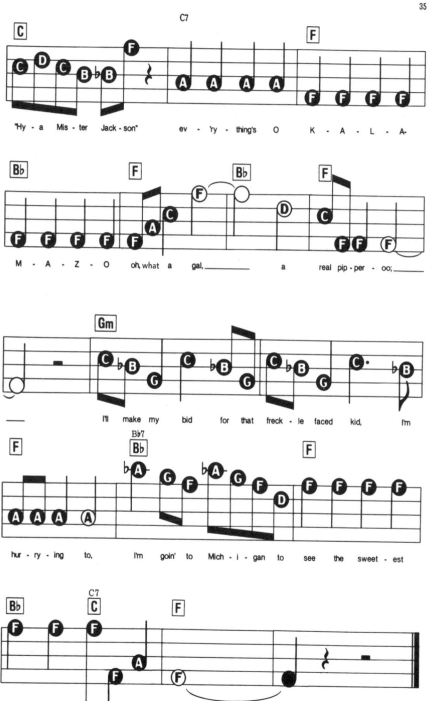

If I Had You

Registration 8
Rhythm: Fox Trot or Swing

Words and Music by Ted Shapiro,
Jimmy Campbell and Reg Connelly

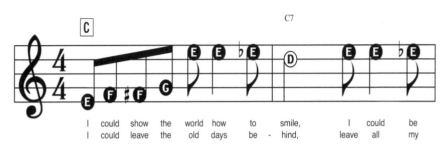

I could show the world how to smile,
I could leave the old days be - hind,

I could be
leave all my

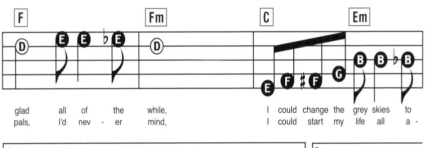

glad all of the while,
pals, I'd nev - er mind,

I could change the grey skies to
I could start my life all a -

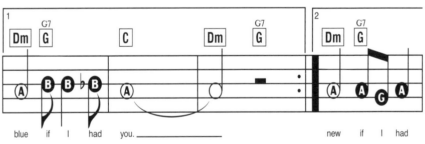

blue if I had you. _____

new if I had

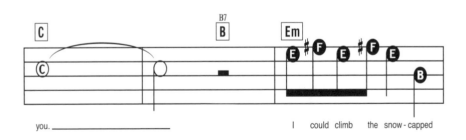

you. _____

I could climb the snow - capped

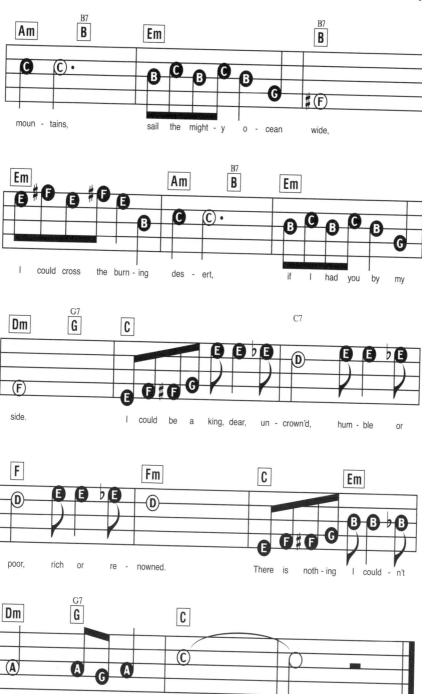

Just You, Just Me

Registration 2
Rhythm: Swing or Fox Trot

Music by Jesse Greer
Lyrics by Raymond Klages

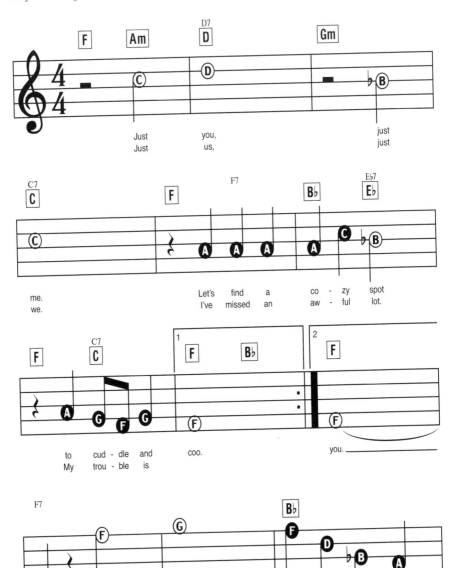

La Vie en Rose
(Take Me to Your Heart Again)

Original French Lyrics by Edith Piaf
Music by Luis Guglielmi
English Lyrics by Mack David

Registration 1
Rhythm: Fox Trot or Ballad

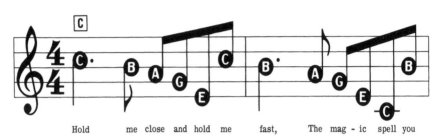

Hold me close and hold me fast, The mag - ic spell you

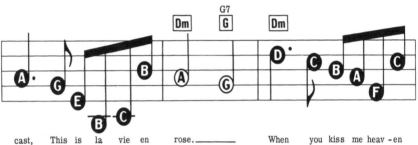

cast, This is la vie en rose._____ When you kiss me heav - en

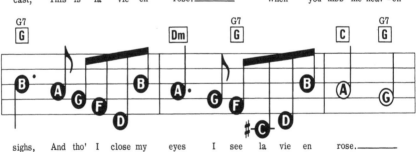

sighs, And tho' I close my eyes I see la vie en rose._____

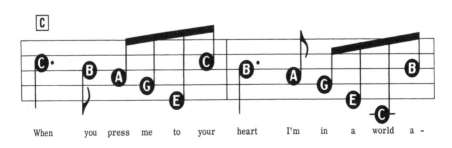

When you press me to your heart I'm in a world a -

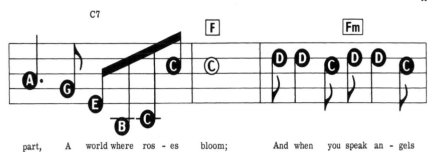

part,   A   world where ros - es   bloom;   And when   you speak an - gels

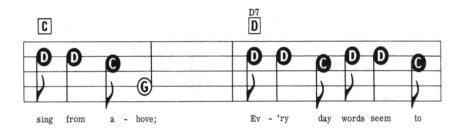

sing   from   a - bove;   Ev - 'ry   day words seem   to

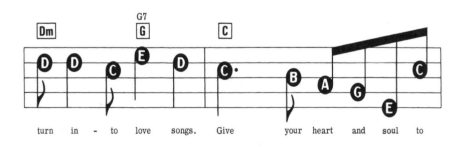

turn   in - to   love   songs.   Give   your   heart   and   soul   to

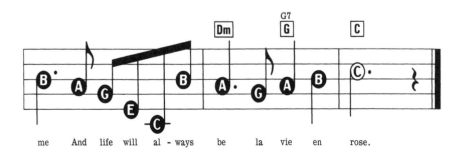

me   And   life   will   al - ways   be   la   vie   en   rose.

Laura

Registration 1
Rhythm: Fox Trot or 8-Beat

Lyrics by Johnny Mercer
Music by David Raksin

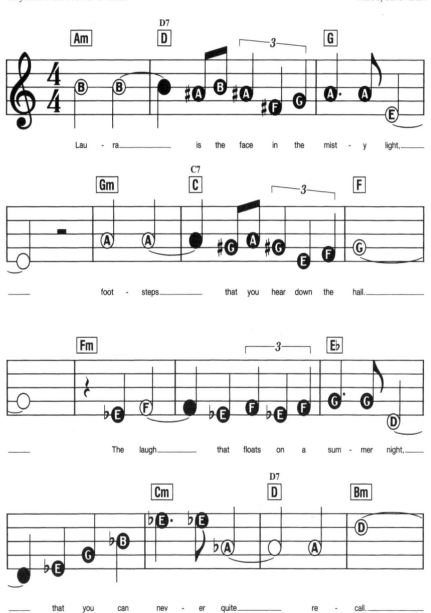

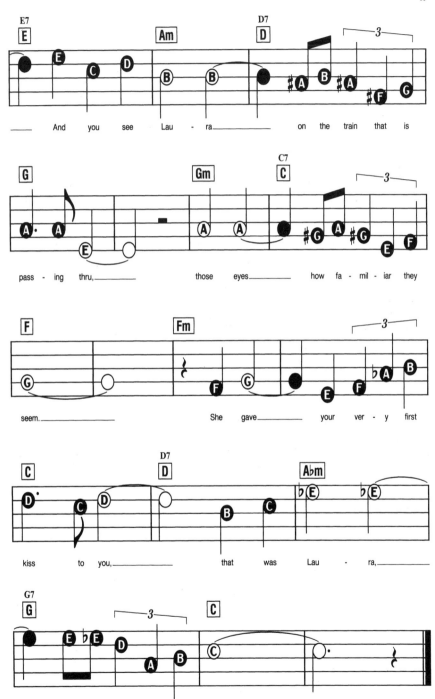

Mack the Knife
from THE THREEPENNY OPERA

Registration 8
Rhythm: Swing

English Words by Marc Blitzstein
Original German Words by Bert Brecht
Music by Kurt Weill

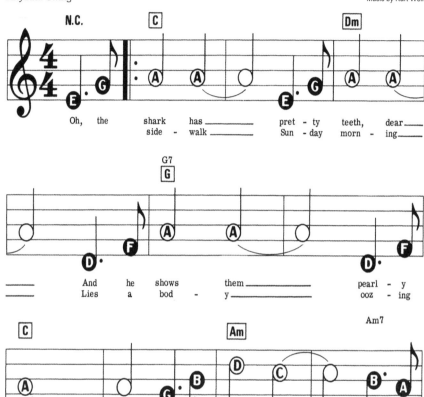

Oh, the shark has _____ pret - ty teeth, dear _____
side - walk _____ Sun - day morn - ing _____

And he shows them _____ pearl - y
Lies a bod - y _____ ooz - ing

white. _____ Just a jack - knife _____ has Mac -
life; _____ Some - one's sneak - ing _____ 'round the

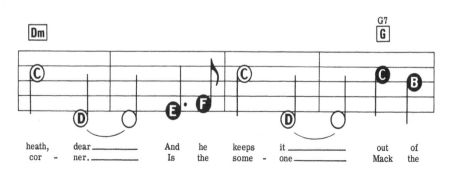

heath, dear _____ And he keeps it _____ out of
cor - ner. _____ Is the some - one _____ Mack the

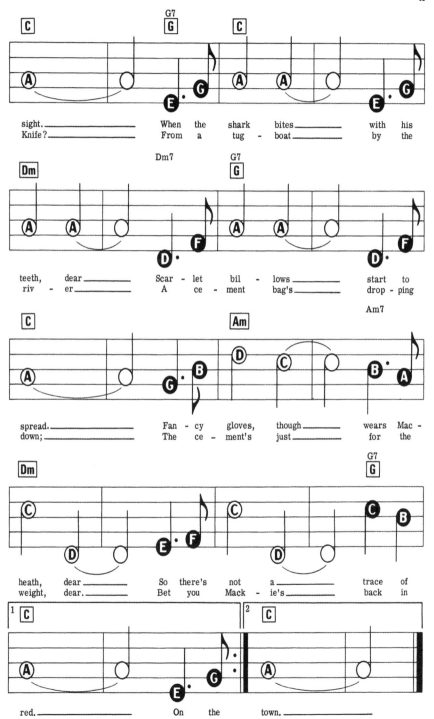

Mambo Italiano

Registration 7
Rhythm: Mambo or Latin

Words and Music by
Bob Merrill

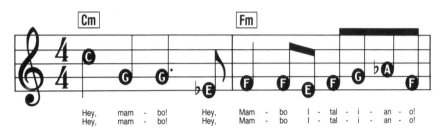

Hey,   mam - bo!   Hey,   Mam - bo   I - tal - i - an - o!
Hey,   mam - bo!   Hey,   Mam - bo   I - tal - i - an - o!

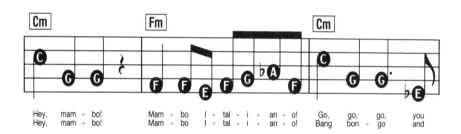

Hey,   mam - bo!   Mam - bo   I - tal - i - an - o!   Go,   go,   go,   you
Hey,   mam - bo!   Mam - bo   I - tal - i - an - o!   Bang   bon - go   and

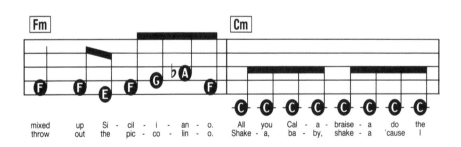

mixed   up   Si - cil - i - an - o.   All   you   Cal - a - braise - a   do   the
throw   out   the   pic - co - lin - o.   Shake - a,   ba - by,   shake - a   'cause   I

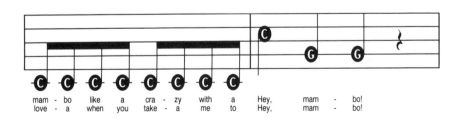

mam - bo   like   a   cra - zy   with   a   Hey,   mam - bo!
love - a   when   you   take - a   me   to   Hey,   mam - bo!

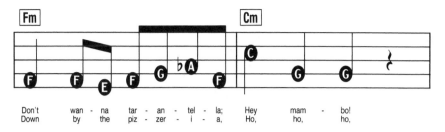

Don't wan - na tar - an - tel - la; Hey mam - bo!
Down by the piz - zer - i - a, Ho, ho, ho,

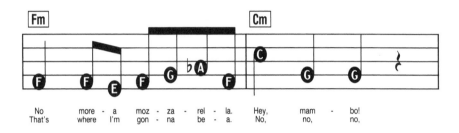

No more - a moz - za - rel - la. Hey, mam - bo!
That's where I'm gon - na be - a. No, no, no,

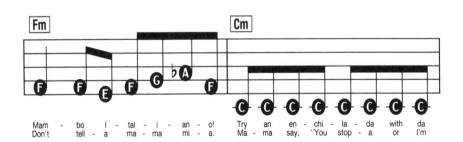

Mam - bo I - tal - i - an - o! Try an en - chi - la - da with da
Don't tell - a ma - ma mi - a. Ma - ma say, "You stop - a or I'm

C7

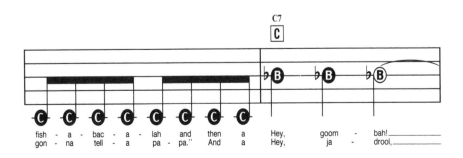

fish - a - bac - a - lah and then a Hey, goom - bah!
gon - na tell - a pa - pa." And a Hey, ja - drool,

48

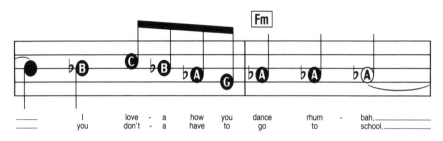

I love - a how you dance rhum - bah,___
you don't - a have to go to school,___

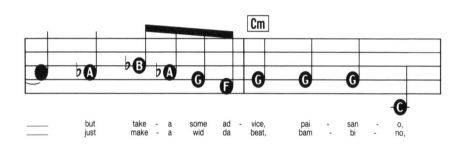

but take - a some ad - vice, pai - san - o,
just make - a wid da beat, bam - bi - no,

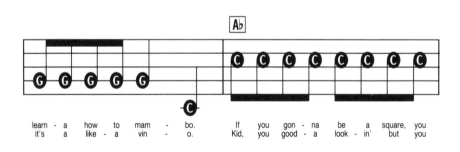

learn - a how to mam - bo. If you gon - na be a square, you
it's a like - a vin - o. Kid, you good - a look - in' but you

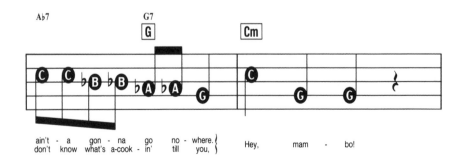

ain't - a gon - na go no - where.
don't know what's a-cook - in' till you, Hey, mam - bo!

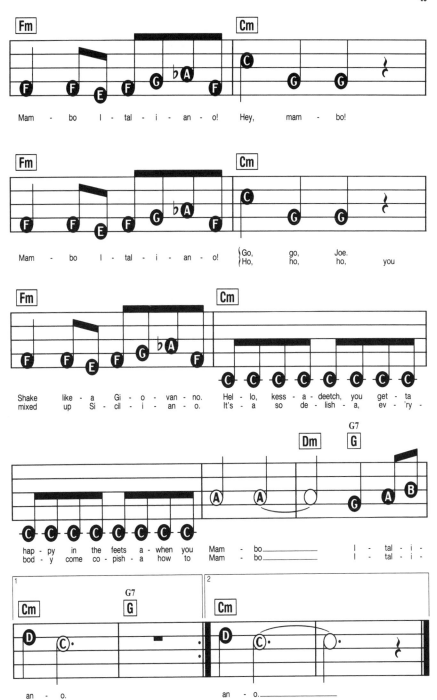

Mr. Bojangles

Registration 3
Rhythm: Waltz

Words and Music by
Jerry Jeff Walker

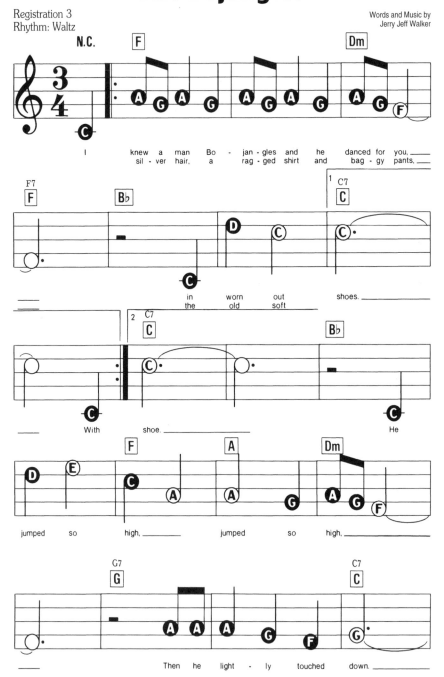

I knew a man Bo - jan - gles and he danced for you, ____
sil - ver hair, a rag - ged shirt and bag - gy pants, ____

in worn out shoes. ____
the old soft ____

With shoe. ____ He

jumped so high, ____ jumped so high, ____

Then he light - ly touched down. ____

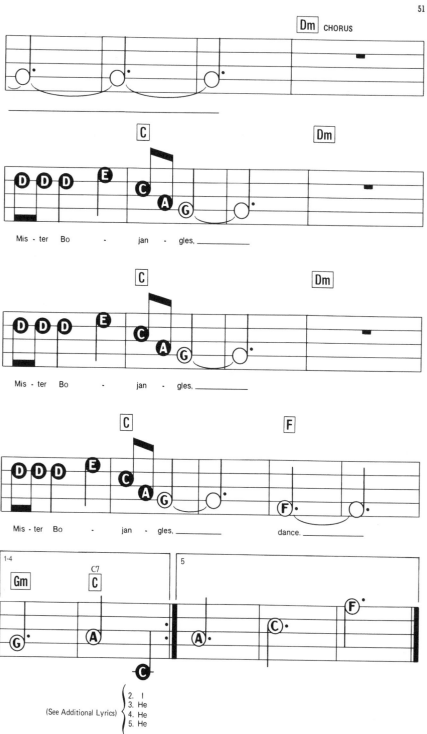

Additional Lyrics

Verse 2   I met him in a cell in New Orleans
I was down and out.
He looked at me to be the eyes of age
As he spoke right out.
He talked of life, talked of life,
He laughed slapped his leg a step.
(Chorus)

Verse 3   He said his name, Bojangles,
Then he danced a lick across the cell.
He grabbed his pants a better stance
Oh, he jumped up high,
He clicked his heels.
He let go a laugh, let go a laugh,
Shook back his clothes all around
(Chorus)

Verse 4   He danced for those at minstrel shows
And county fairs throughout the South.
He spoke with tears of fifteen years
How his dog and he traveled about.
His dog up and died, he up and died,
After twenty years he still grieved.
(Chorus)

Verse 5   He said, "I dance now at every chance
In honky tonks for drinks and tips.
But most of the time I spend behind these county bars."
He said, "I drinks a bit."
He shook his head
And as he shook his head, I heard someone ask please
(Chorus)

Theme from "New York, New York"

from NEW YORK, NEW YORK

Registration 4
Rhythm: Swing

Words by Fred Ebb
Music by John Kander

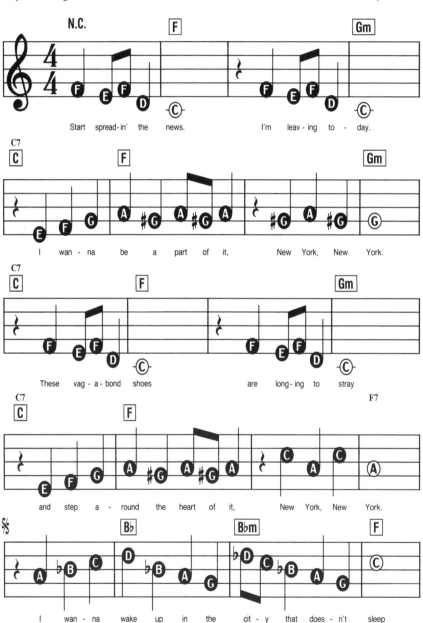

54

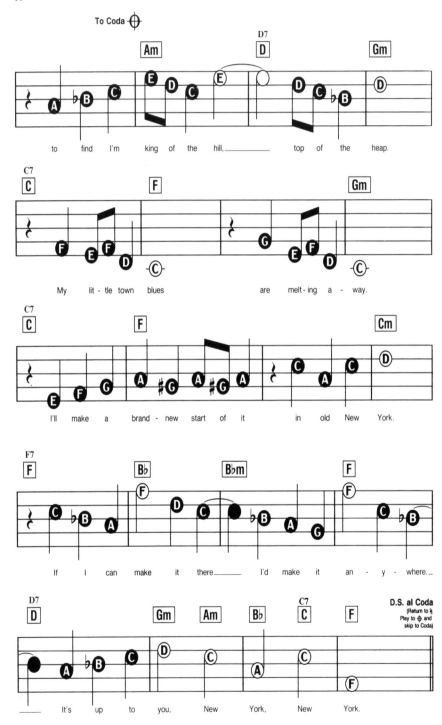

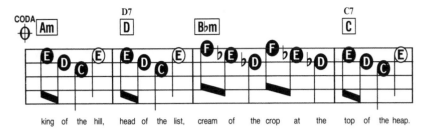

king of the hill, head of the list, cream of the crop at the top of the heap.

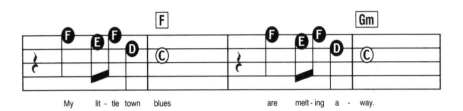

My lit - tle town blues are melt - ing a - way.

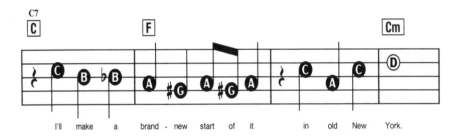

I'll make a brand - new start of it in old New York.

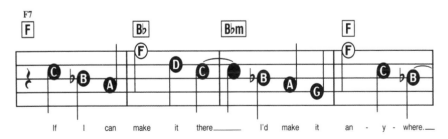

If I can make it there____ I'd make it an - y - where.____

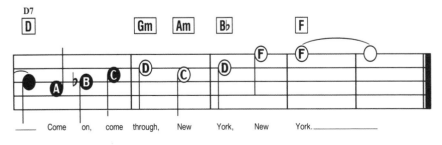

____ Come on, come through, New York, New York.____

On Broadway

Registration 1
Rhythm: Fox Trot

Words and Music by Barry Mann,
Cynthia Weil, Mike Stoller and Jerry Leiber

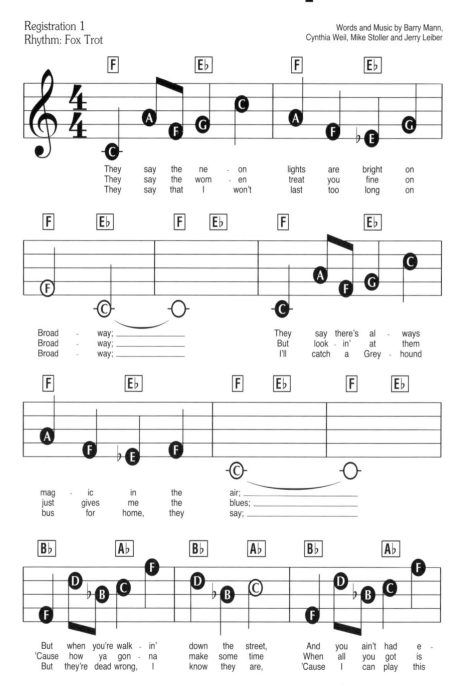

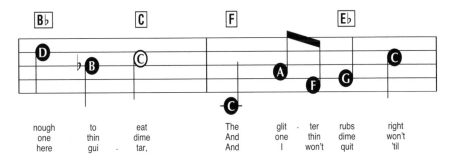

nough to eat The glit - ter rubs right
one thin dime And one thin dime won't
here gui - tar, And I won't quit 'til

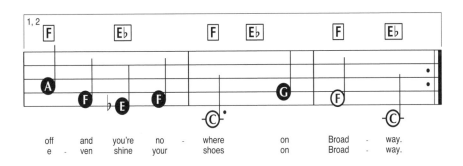

off and you're no - where on Broad - way.
e - ven shine your shoes on Broad - way.

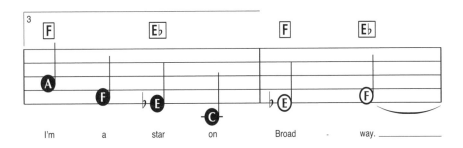

I'm a star on Broad - way.

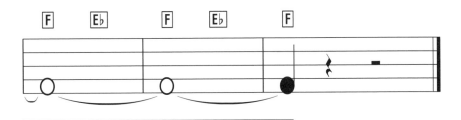

Over the Rainbow
from THE WIZARD OF OZ

Registration 5
Rhythm: Ballad

Music by Harold Arlen
Lyric by E.Y. "Yip" Harburg

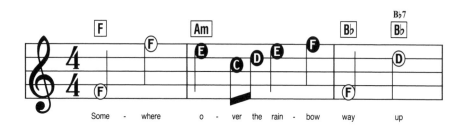

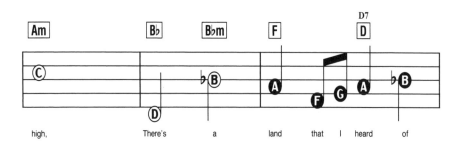

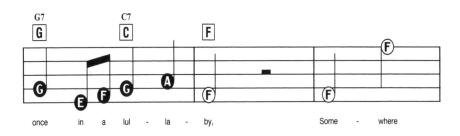

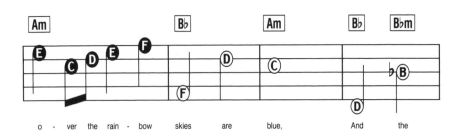

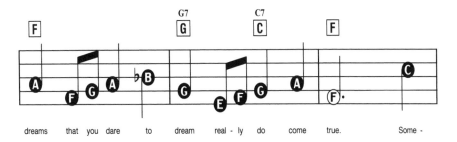

dreams that you dare to dream real - ly do come true. Some -

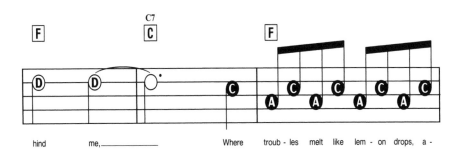

day I'll wish up - on a star and wake up where the clouds are far be -

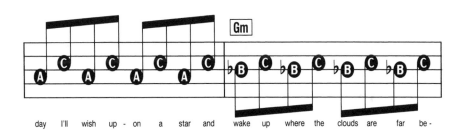

hind me,_____ Where troub - les melt like lem - on drops, a -

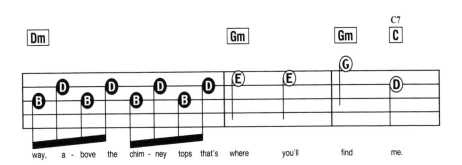

way, a - bove the chim - ney tops that's where you'll find me.

60

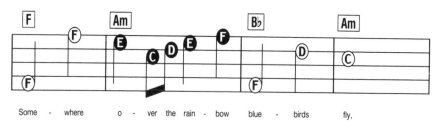

Some - where   o - ver the rain - bow   blue - birds   fly,

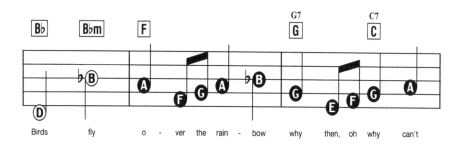

Birds   fly   o - ver the rain - bow   why   then, oh why   can't

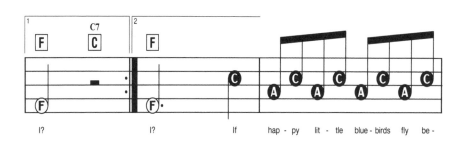

I?   I?   If   hap - py   lit - tle   blue - birds   fly   be -

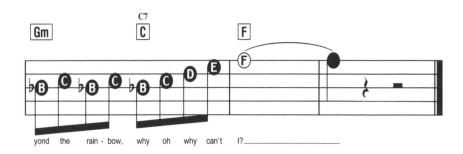

yond   the   rain - bow,   why   oh   why   can't   I?

Pieces of Dreams
(Little Boy Lost)
from the Motion Picture PIECES OF DREAMS

Registration 8
Rhythm: Fox Trot or Swing

Lyrics by Alan and Marilyn Bergman
Music by Michel Legrand

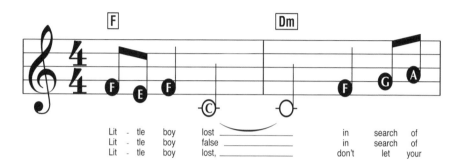

Lit - tle boy lost _____ in search of
Lit - tle boy false _____ in search of
Lit - tle boy lost, _____ don't let your

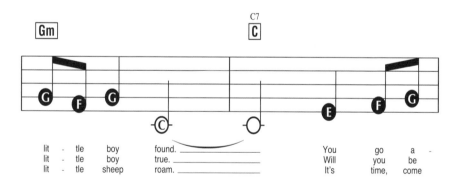

lit - tle boy found. _____ You go a -
lit - tle boy true. _____ Will you be
lit - tle sheep roam. _____ It's time, come

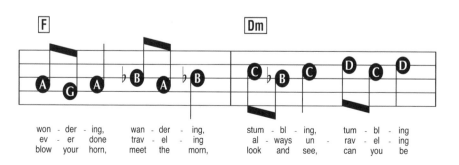

won - der - ing, wan - der - ing, stum - bl - ing, tum - bl - ing
ev - er done trav - el - ing al - ways un - rav - el - ing
blow your horn, meet the morn, look and see, can you be

62

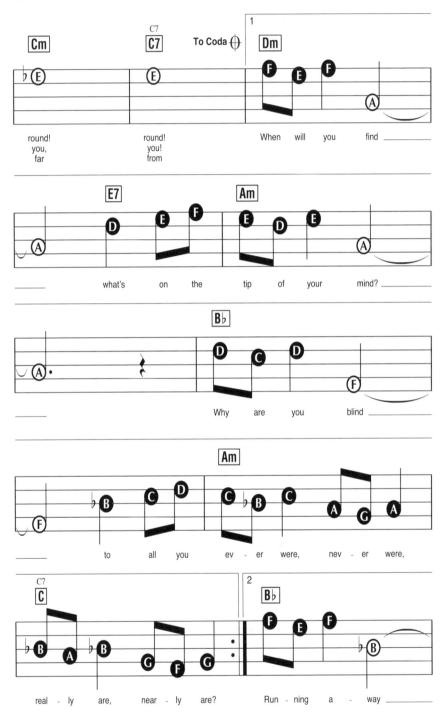

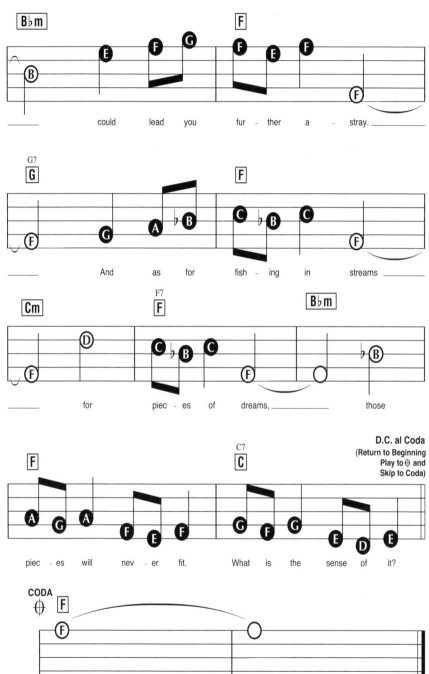

September in the Rain

Registration 3
Rhythm: Ballad or Fox Trot

Words by Al Dubin
Music by Harry Warren

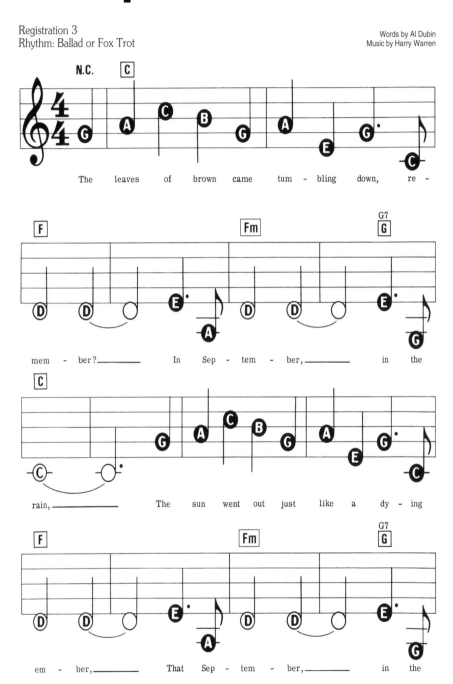

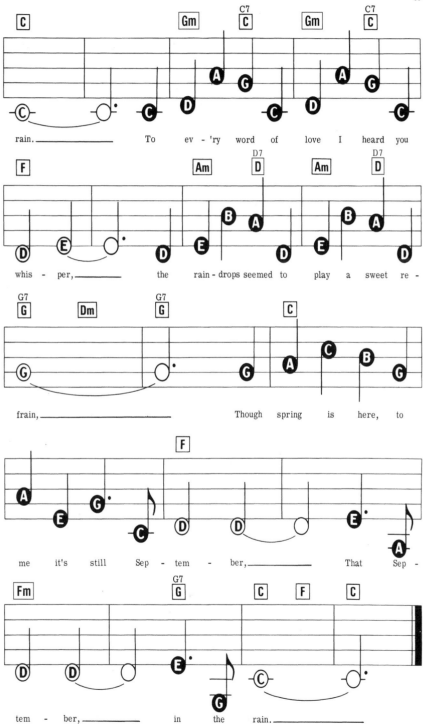

rain. _____ To ev - 'ry word of love I heard you whis - per, _____ the rain - drops seemed to play a sweet re - frain, _____ Though spring is here, to me it's still Sep - tem - ber, _____ That Sep - tem - ber, _____ in the rain. _____

The Shadow of Your Smile
Love Theme from THE SANDPIPER

Registration 4
Rhythm: Bossa Nova or Latin

Music by Johnny Mandel
Words by Paul Francis Webster

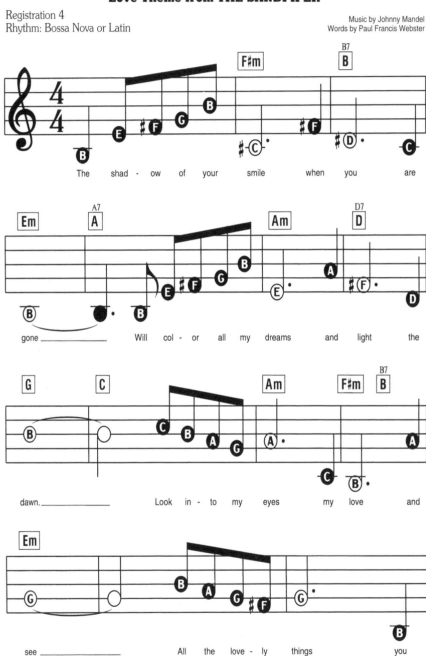

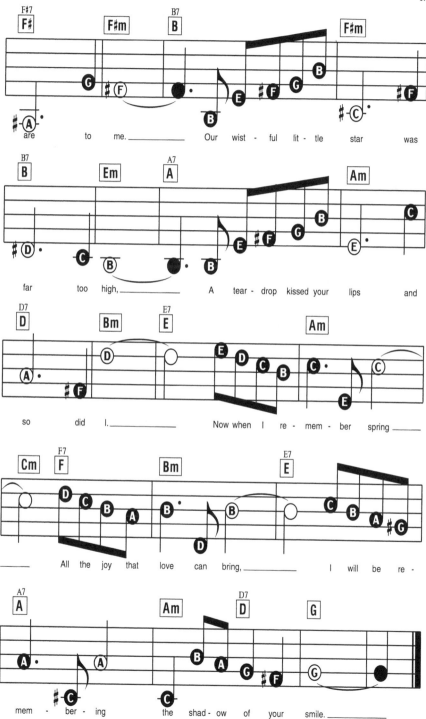

Sing, Sing, Sing

Registration 4
Rhythm: Swing

Words and Music by
Louis Prima

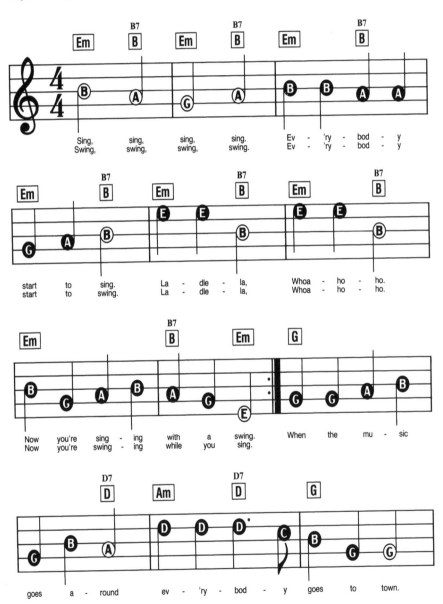

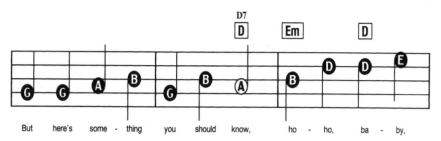

But here's some - thing you should know, ho - ho, ba - by,

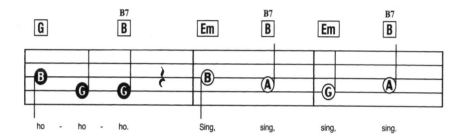

ho - ho - ho. Sing, sing, sing, sing.

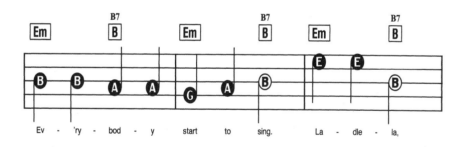

Ev - 'ry - bod - y start to sing. La - dle - la,

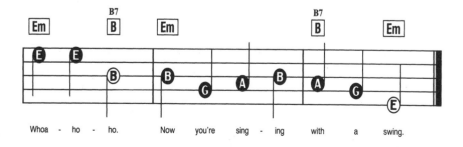

Whoa - ho - ho. Now you're sing - ing with a swing.

Someone to Watch Over Me

Registration 7
Rhythm: Ballad or Swing

Music and Lyrics by George Gershwin
and Ira Gershwin

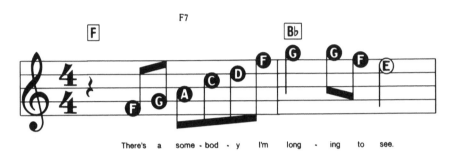

There's a some - bod - y I'm long - ing to see.

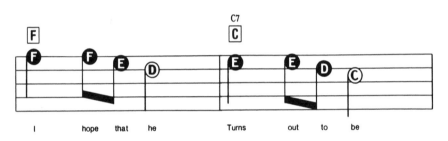

I hope that he Turns out to be

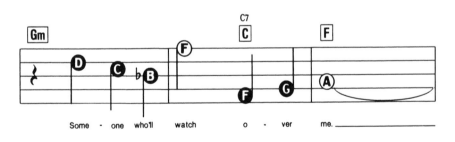

Some - one who'll watch o - ver me. ____

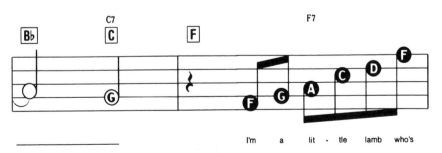

I'm a lit - tle lamb who's

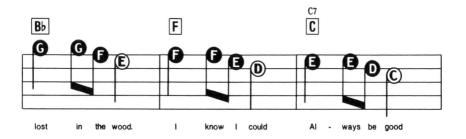

lost in the wood. I know I could Al - ways be good

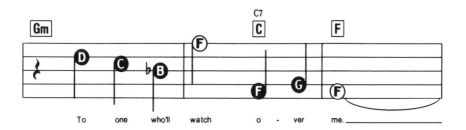

To one who'll watch o - ver me.

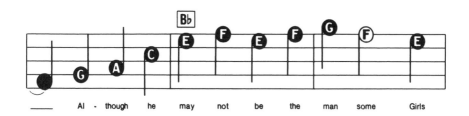

Al - though he may not be the man some Girls

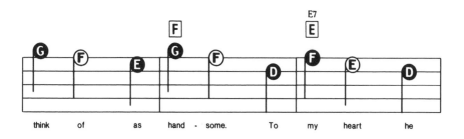

think of as hand - some. To my heart he

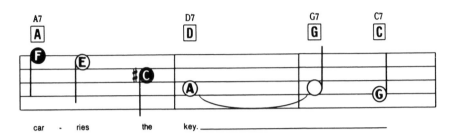

car - ries the key.

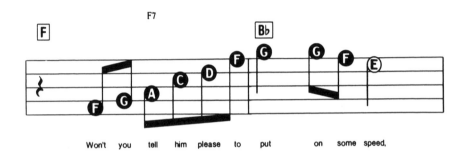

Won't you tell him please to put on some speed,

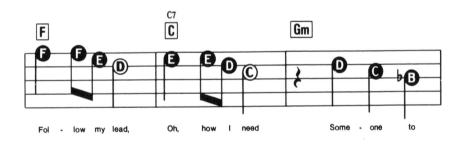

Fol - low my lead, Oh, how I need Some - one to

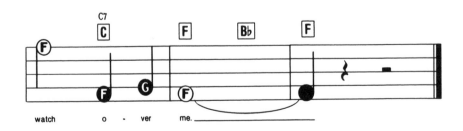

watch o - ver me.

Something's Gotta Give

Registration 5
Rhythm: Fox Trot or Swing

Words and Music by
Johnny Mercer

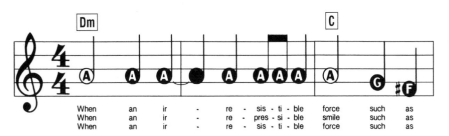

When an ir - re - sis - ti - ble force such as
When an ir - re - pres - si - ble smile such as
When an ir - re - sis - ti - ble force such as

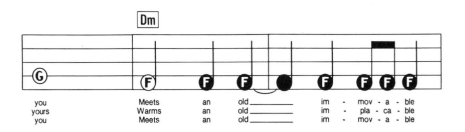

you Meets an old_____ im - mov - a - ble
yours Warms an old_____ im - pla - ca - ble
you Meets an old_____ im - mov - a - ble

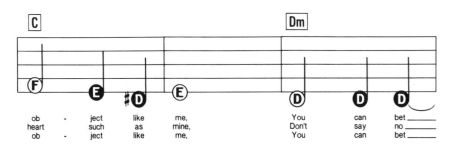

ob - ject like me, You can bet_____
heart such as mine, Don't say no_____
ob - ject like me, You can bet_____

To Coda

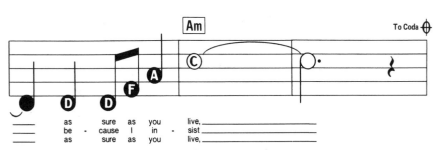

_____ as sure as you live, _____
_____ be - cause I in - sist _____
_____ as sure as you live, _____

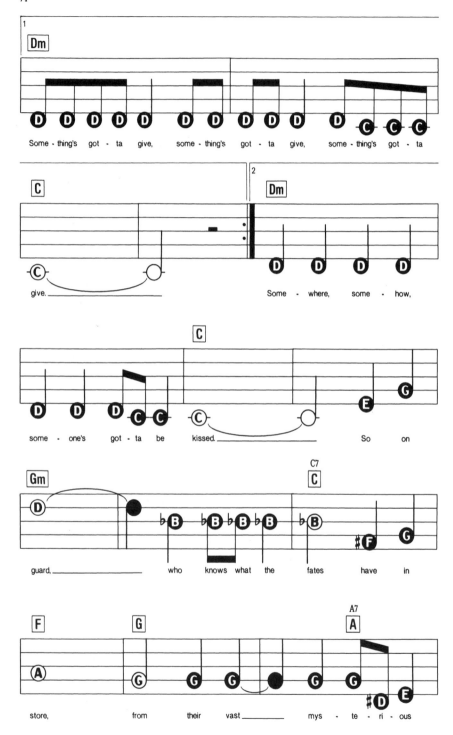

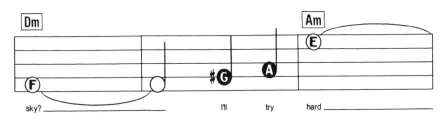

sky? _____ I'll try hard _____

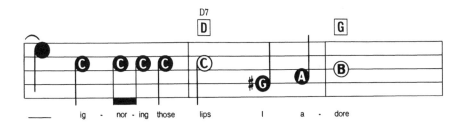

____ ig - nor - ing those lips I a - dore

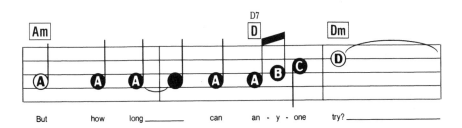

But how long _____ can an - y - one try? _____

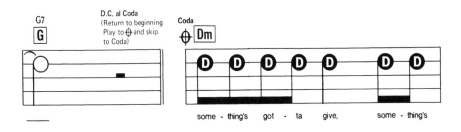

D.C. al Coda
(Return to beginning
Play to ⊕ and skip
to Coda)

Coda

____ some - thing's got - ta give, some - thing's

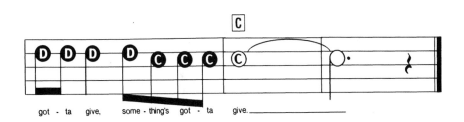

got - ta give, some - thing's got - ta give. _____

Stand by Your Man

Registration 3
Rhythm: Country or Shuffle

Words and Music by Tammy Wynette
and Billy Sherrill

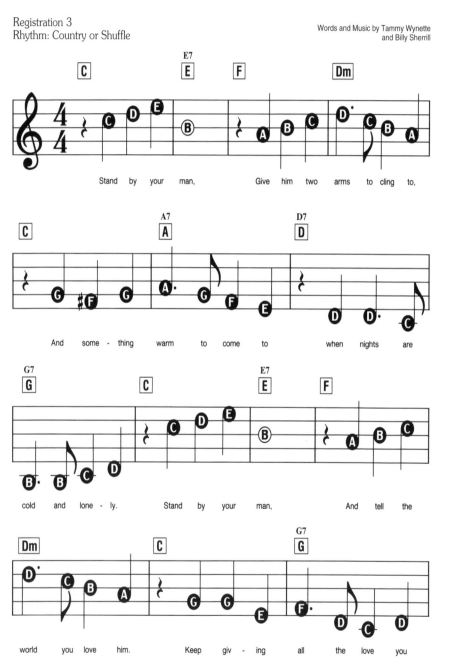

77

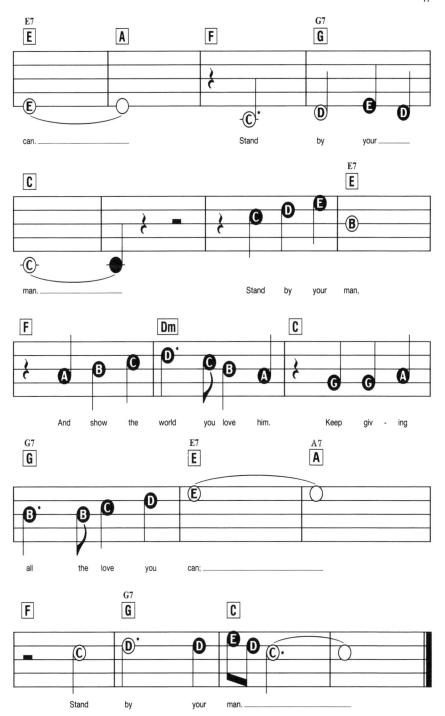

Stars Fell on Alabama

Registration 1
Rhythm: Swing or Ballad

Words by Mitchell Parish
Music by Frank Perkins

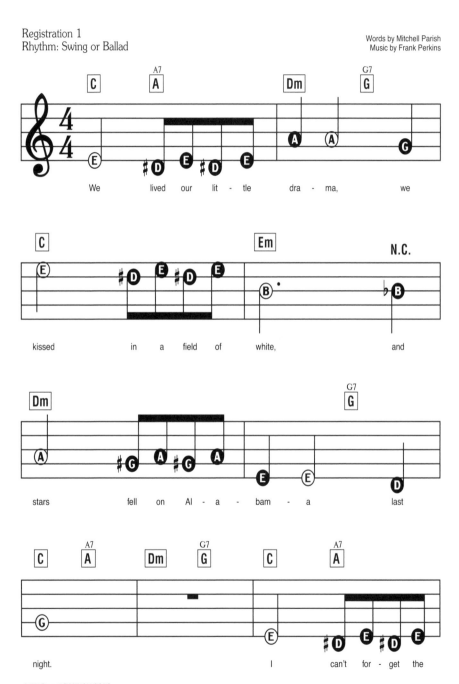

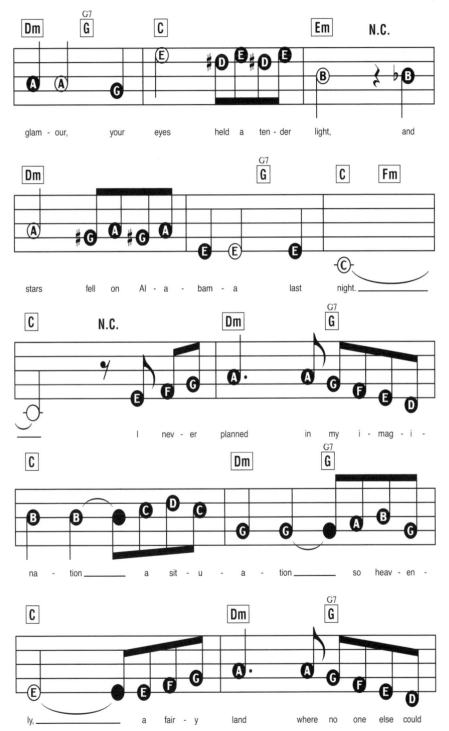

80

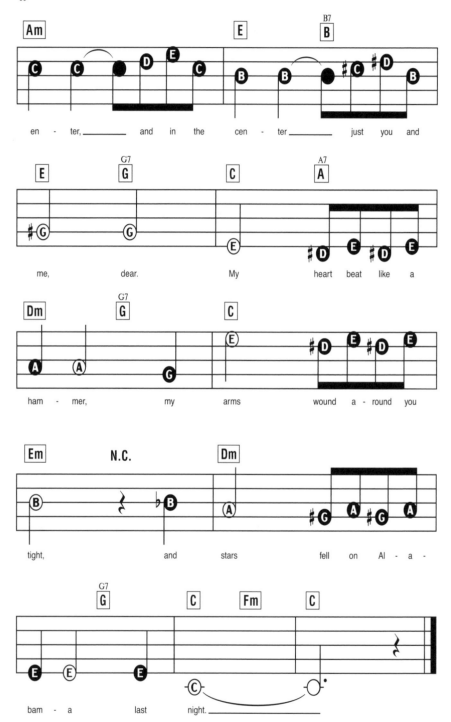

Try a Little Tenderness

Registration 1
Rhythm: Swing or Ballad

Words and Music by Harry Woods,
Jimmy Campbell and Reg Connelly

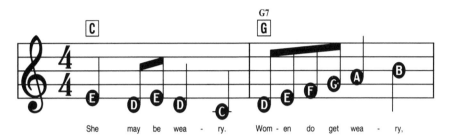

She   may   be   wea - ry.   Wom - en   do   get   wea - ry,

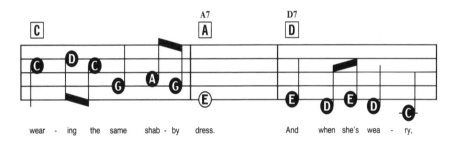

wear - ing   the   same   shab - by   dress.   And   when she's   wea - ry,

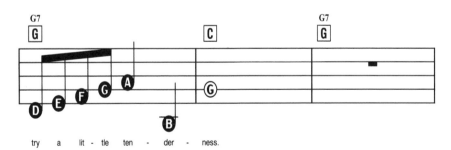

try   a   lit - tle   ten - der - ness.

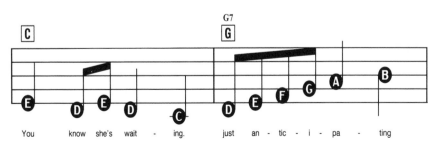

You   know she's   wait - ing.   just   an - tic - i - pa - ting

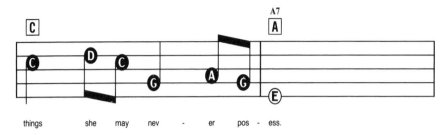

things she may nev - er pos - ess.

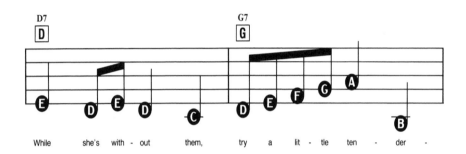

While she's with - out them, try a lit - tle ten - der -

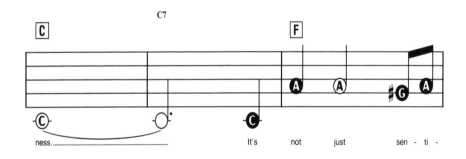

ness. It's not just sen - ti -

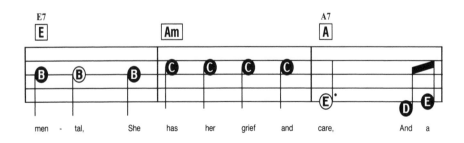

men - tal, She has her grief and care, And a

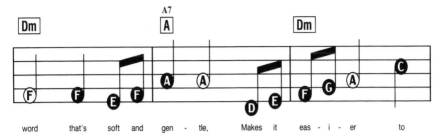

word   that's   soft   and   gen - tle,   Makes   it   eas - i - er   to

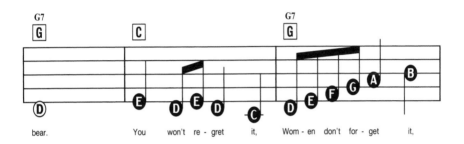

bear.   You   won't re - gret   it,   Wom - en   don't   for - get   it,

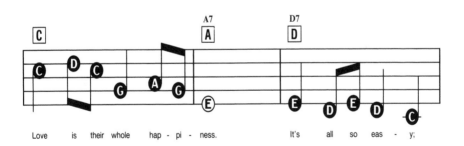

Love   is   their   whole   hap - pi - ness.   It's   all   so   eas - y;

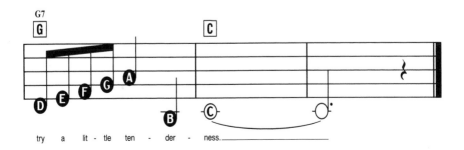

try   a   lit - tle   ten - der - ness.

Song from M*A*S*H
(Suicide Is Painless)

Registration 5
Rhythm: Rock

Words and Music by Mike Altman
and Johnny Mandel

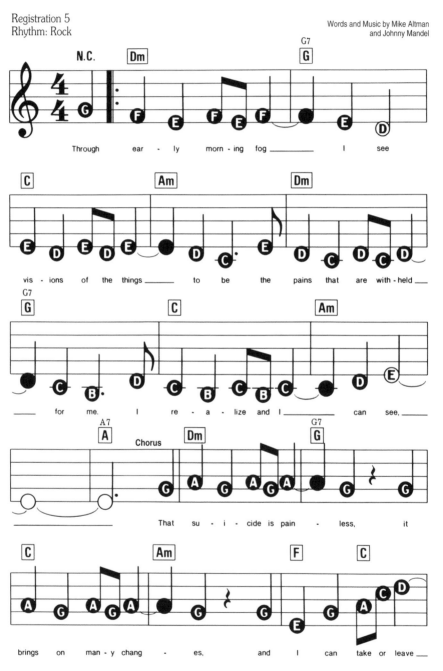

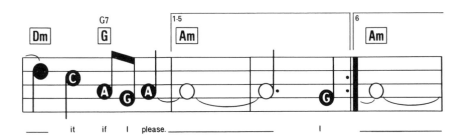

it   if   I   please.   I

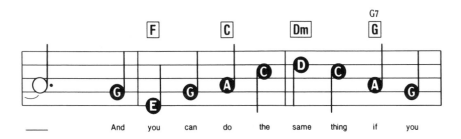

And   you   can   do   the   same   thing   if   you

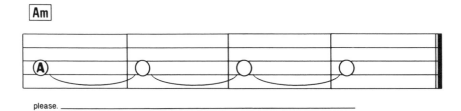

please.

Additional Lyrics

2. I try to find a way to make
All our little joys relate
Without that ever present hate
But now I know that it's too late.
And *Chorus*

3. The game of life is hard to play,
I'm going to lose it anyway,
The losing card I'll someday lay
So this is all I have to say;
That *Chorus*

4. The only way to win, is cheat
And lay it down before I'm beat,
And to another give a seat
For that's the only painless feat.
'Cause *Chorus*

5. The sword of time will pierce our skins,
It doesn't hurt when it begins,
But as it works its way on in,
The pain grows stronger, watch it grin.
For *Chorus*

6. A brave man once requested me
To answer questions that are key,
Is it to be or not to be
And I replied; "Oh, why ask me."
'Cause *Chorus*

Summer Wind

Registration 7
Rhythm: Swing

English Words by Johnny Mercer
Original German Lyrics by Hans Bradtke
Music by Henry Mayer

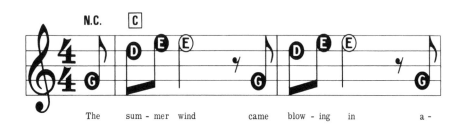

The sum - mer wind came blow - ing in a -

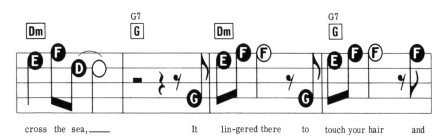

cross the sea, ___ It lin-gered there to touch your hair and

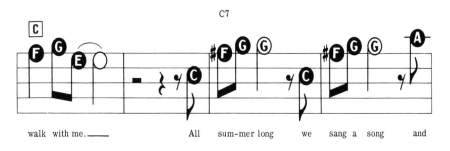

walk with me. ___ All sum-mer long we sang a song and

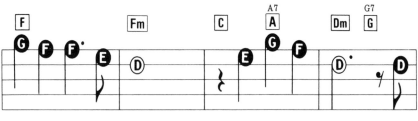

strolled the gold - en sand, Two sweet-hearts and the

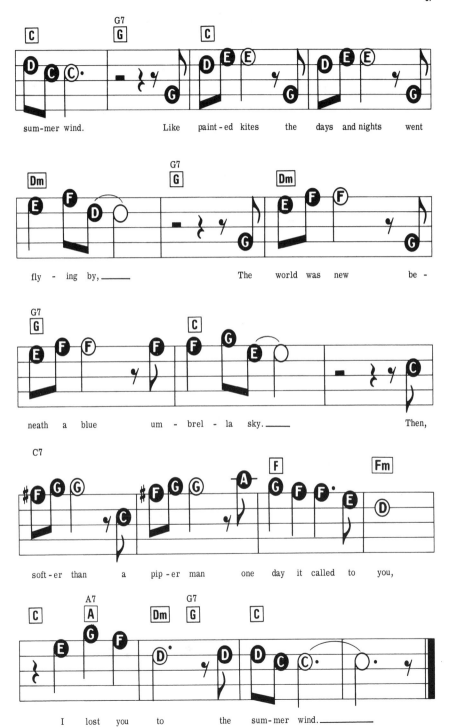

Sweet Georgia Brown

Registration 7
Rhythm: Fox Trot or Swing

Words and Music by Ben Bernie,
Maceo Pinkard and Kenneth Casey

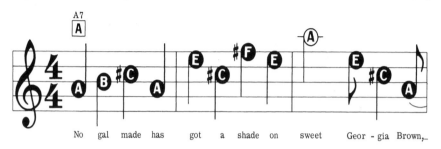

No gal made has got a shade on sweet Geor - gia Brown,_

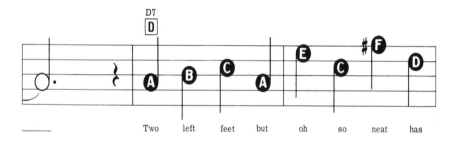

_____ Two left feet but oh so neat has

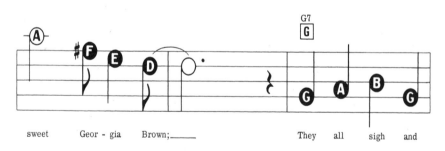

sweet Geor - gia Brown;_____ They all sigh and

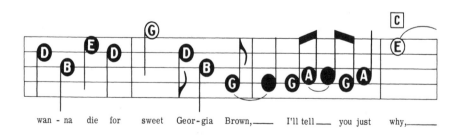

wan - na die for sweet Geor-gia Brown,_____ I'll tell ___ you just why,_____

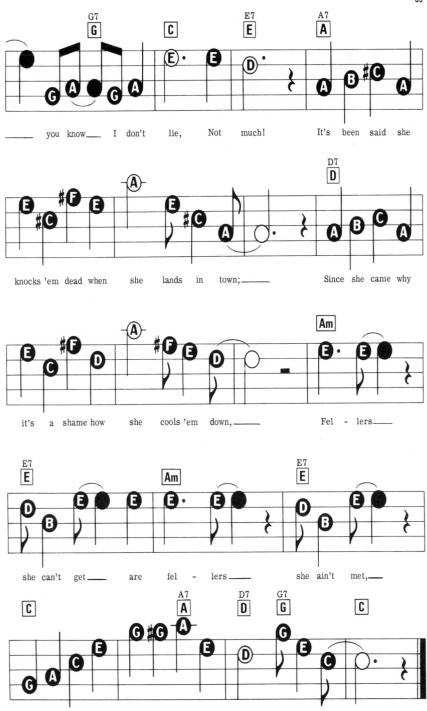

Tea for Two

Registration 8
Rhythm: Shuffle or Swing

Words by Irving Caesar
Music by Vincent Youmans

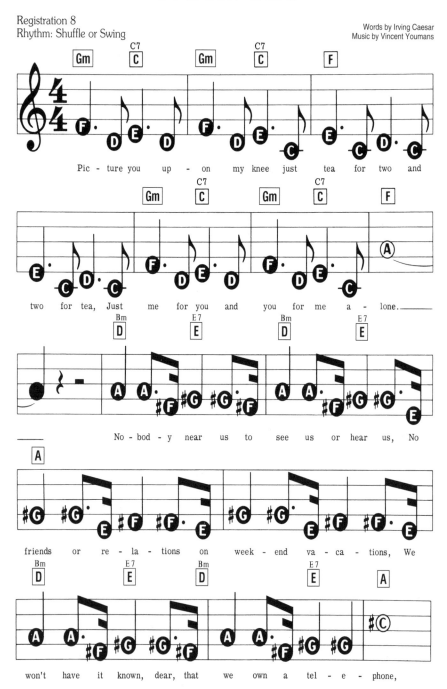

Pic - ture you up - on my knee just tea for two and two for tea, Just me for you and you for me a - lone.

No - bod - y near us to see us or hear us, No friends or re - la - tions on week - end va - ca - tions, We won't have it known, dear, that we own a tel - e - phone,

91

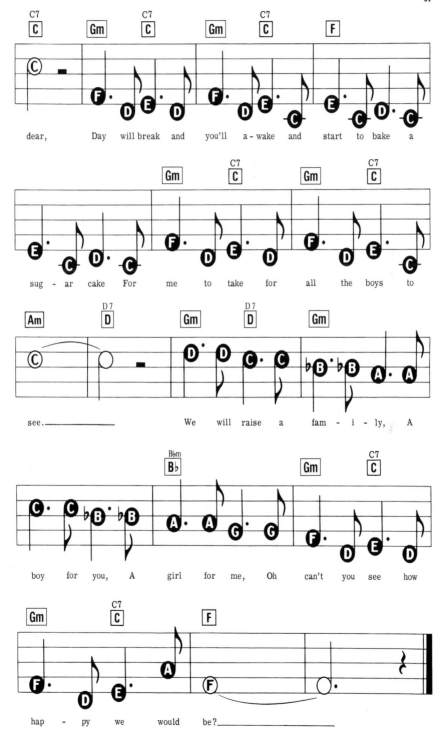

Tender Is the Night

Registration 1
Rhythm: Swing or Ballad

Words by Paul Francis Webster
Music by Sammy Fain

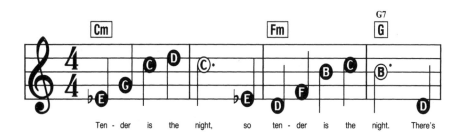

Ten - der is the night, so ten - der is the night. There's

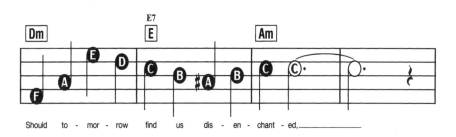

no one in the world ex - cept the two of us.

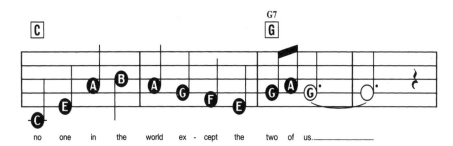

Should to - mor - row find us dis - en - chant - ed,

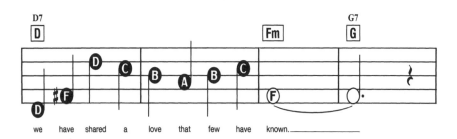

we have shared a love that few have known.

93

The Trolley Song
from MEET ME IN ST. LOUIS

Registration 4
Rhythm: Swing

Words and Music by Hugh Martin
and Ralph Blane

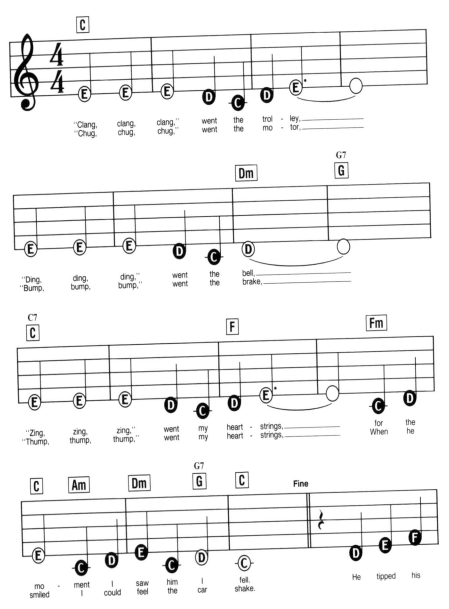

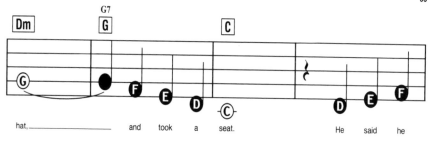

hat,_____ and took a seat. He said he

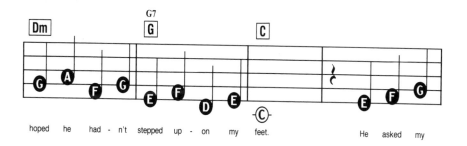

hoped he had - n't stepped up - on my feet. He asked my

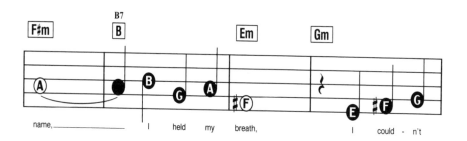

name,_____ I held my breath, I could - n't

D.C. al Fine
(Return to beginning
Play to Fine)

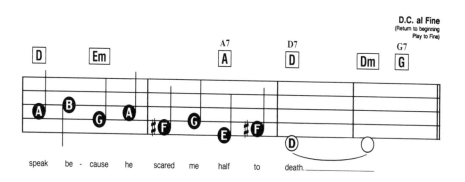

speak be - cause he scared me half to death._____

What Is This Thing Called Love?

Registration 7
Rhythm: Fox Trot or Swing

Words and Music by
Cole Porter

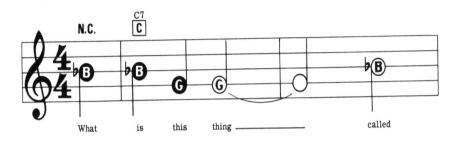

What   is   this   thing _____ called

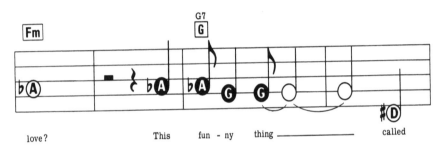

love?   This   fun - ny   thing _____ called

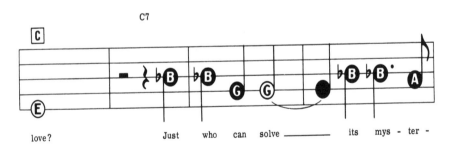

love?   Just   who   can   solve _____ its   mys - ter -

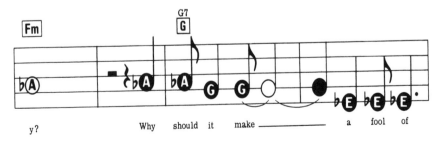

y?   Why   should   it   make _____ a   fool   of

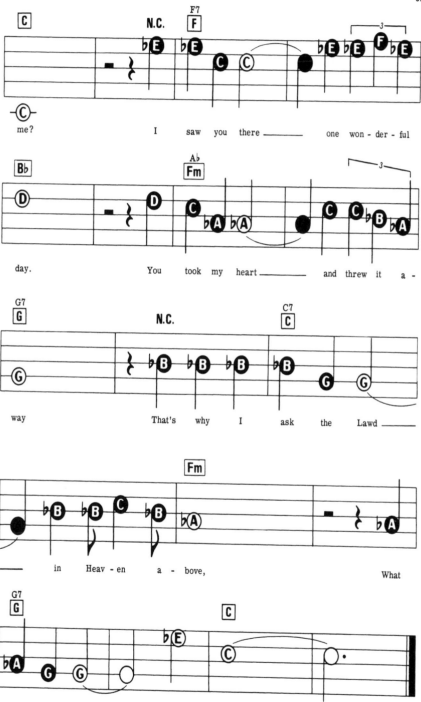

The Wind Beneath My Wings

Registration 3
Rhythm: Rock

Words and Music by Larry Henley
and Jeff Silbar

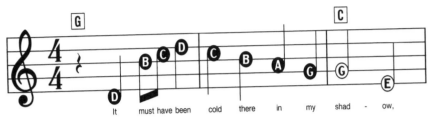

It must have been cold there in my shad - ow,

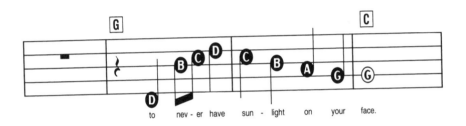

to nev - er have sun - light on your face.

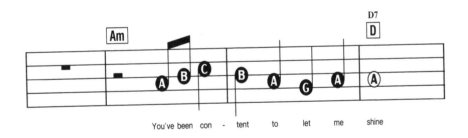

You've been con - tent to let me shine

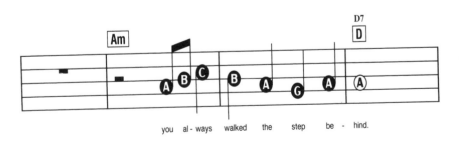

you al - ways walked the step be - hind.

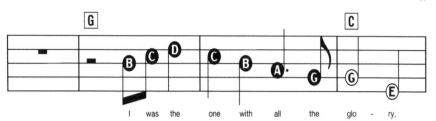

I was the one with all the glo - ry,

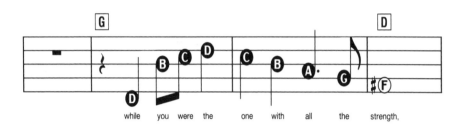

while you were the one with all the strength,

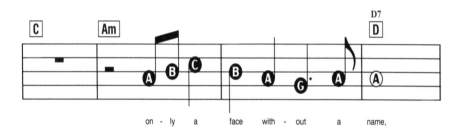

on - ly a face with - out a name,

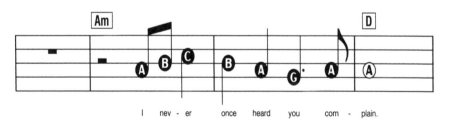

I nev - er once heard you com - plain.

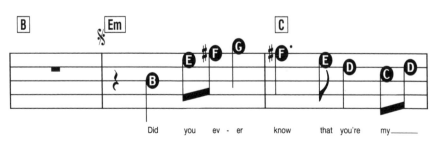

Did you ev - er know that you're my____

100

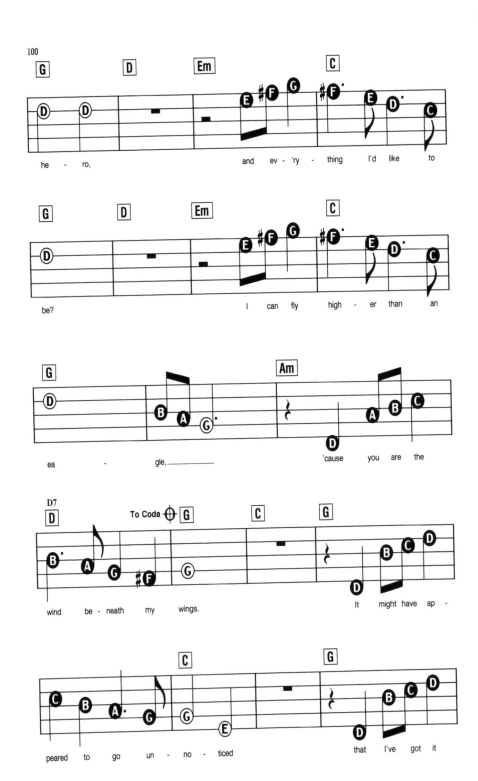

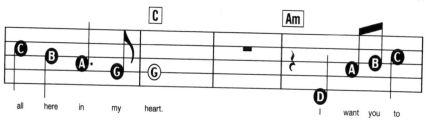

all   here   in   my   heart.   I   want   you   to

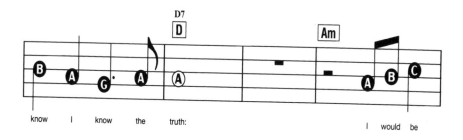

know   I   know   the   truth: I   would   be

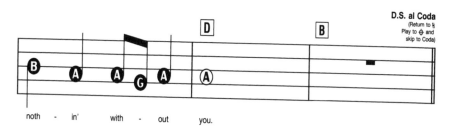

noth - in'   with - out   you.

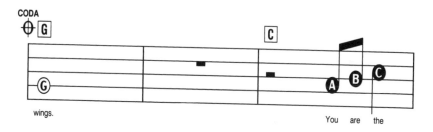

wings.   You   are   the

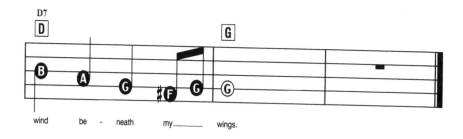

wind   be - neath   my___   wings.

What You Won't Do for Love

Registration 1
Rhythm: Funk or Rock

Words and Music by Bobby Caldwell
and Alfons Kettner

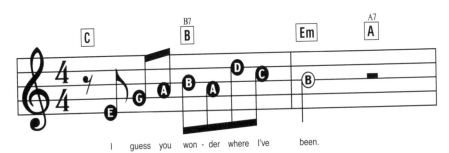

I guess you won - der where I've been.

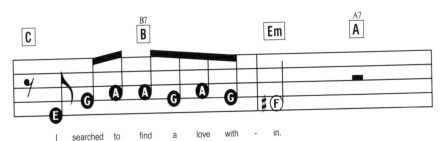

I searched to find a love with - in.

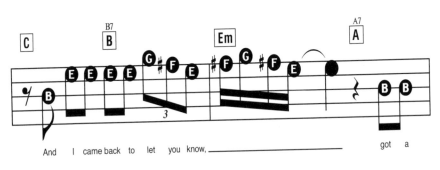

And I came back to let you know, _____ got a

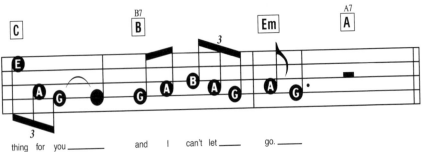

thing for you _____ and I can't let _____ go. _____

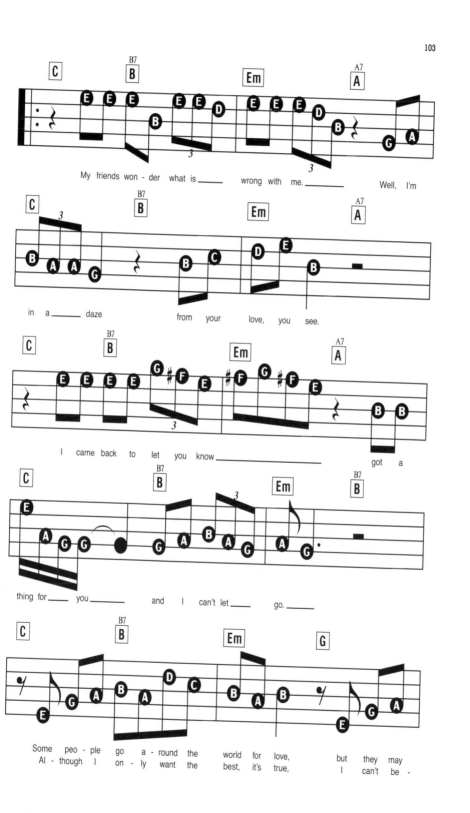

My friends won - der what is _____ wrong with me. _____ Well, I'm

in a _____ daze   from your   love,   you   see.

I came back to   let you know _____   got a

thing for _____ you _____   and   I can't let _____   go. _____

Some peo - ple   go a - round the   world for   love,   but   they may
Al - though I   on - ly want the   best,   it's   true,   I   can't be -

104

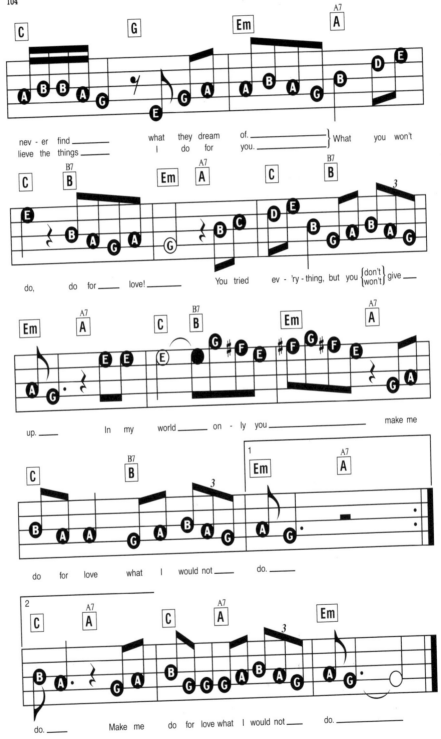